HOW WE WENT TO WAR

Deptford & Lewisham 1939-1945

The People's Story

by Lewis Blake

With reminiscences contributed by Age Exchange Reminiscence Centre

ISBN No: 0-901637-75-0

Published by London Borough of Lewisham Arts and Library Service

Contents

"Good Night Children, Everywhere"

[The title of a ballad composed in 1939 "with a tender thought to all evacuated children"]

Monday, 4 September 1939 was to be 'back to school' day for local pupils after the summer holidays. That, at least, is what they thought when the schools 'broke up' in July. But Hitler had other plans. The war-clouds grew darker throughout the summer months, until on Friday, 1 September the Nazis invaded Poland and war became inevitable. The signal was given for the immediate evacuation of schools in London and other major cities to places of greater safety from air attack. Within hours the biggest civilian exodus in British history went into top gear.

A CLASH OF CULTURES

A Devon foster-mother was encouraging a London boy to show more appreciation for the kindnesses he received. He retorted, **"I tell you what it is, lady. You've got all the manners, we've got all the brains"**.

As early as 7.00 am on that warm and sunny Friday the first groups of children, with their teachers and adult helpers, began assembling in school playgrounds throughout Deptford and Lewisham. Most schools were within walking distance of their designated departure stations, but a few needed special buses or trams to take them. Soon the streets filled with long columns of children trudging along the first leg of a journey which would take them they knew not where.

Festooned with identification labels and encumbered by gas masks, haversacks, hold-alls and suitcases, they plodded along, best foot forward. Railway stations beckoned them: up Downham Way to Grove Park; over the bridge to Catford; along the tramtrack to Forest Hill; from every side to Hither Green; from east and west to New Cross and New Cross Gate.... Ladywell, Brockley, Sydenham, Bellingham, Lewisham, Honor Oak - one and all they stood by to receive a human tidal wave.

Small groups of parents and neighbours gathered on corners to wave the evacuees good bye - parents were not permitted on platforms for last farewells. The onlookers seemed more upset than the children. Parties of

The Government attempts to stem the flow of returning evacuees.

Evacuees with their gasmasks add a certain poignancy to this idyllic, rural scene.

Woodyates Road, Lee ARP Post, with poster on the wall saying that children are safer in the country.

senior girls giggled self-consciously as they hurried along. Senior boys affected a show of nonchalance. Mixed juniors seemed to think it was an adventurous day out, though some looked solemn or apprehensive. Those 'in the infants' were the ones most likely to dawdle, to want to turn back, to cry....

War was not supposed to be like this. It was brave soldiers who marched off to war, with bands playing, standards flying, and crowds cheering. But this was a People's War, and here, just to prove its topsy-turviness, the little ones were going away, leaving the grown-ups at home to face the enemy's fire - and to fret for the welfare of the children they might not live to see again.

A CLASH OF CULTURES

"How do you spell 'snarf'?" an evacuee asked his foster-mother. She was at a complete loss. He wanted to write home to say, **"Snarf quiet round here".**

OUT OF SIGHT - BUT NOT OUT OF MIND

40,000 local school children had been registered by their parents for evacuation under the official scheme. Plans were therefore laid down with this number in mind, plus a 10 per cent loading for teachers and welfare workers, making 44,000 in all. Then there were the other categories eligible for evacuation - mothers with pre-school infants, the infirm, the blind, the crippled, and chronically ill hospital patients.

In the event fewer children than expected turned up, some parents having changed their minds, while others made their own private arrangements. Yet the majority of Deptford and Lewisham children vanished from sight in the course of two days. They left a strange gap in the life of the community. Those who remained had no schools to attend, for the teachers had left, too, and the buildings were taken over by the ARP (Air Raid Precautions) and other organisations related to the war.

Friendly in one place, unfriendly in another

I have to go back to the middle of June 1944. That was when the Germans sent the flying bombs over London. I had a baby girl and a small boy and after about a week of trying to cope, I put my name down for evacuation. In a train full of evacuees, we arrived at Halifax, Yorkshire. I was billeted with a friendly lady Grace, and her daughter Jenny. I was quite happy with them for about six months until Jenny was expecting a baby and my room was needed. I was then evacuated to a village in Derbyshire where the atmosphere was far from friendly. I seem to remember that when the weather was right I spent as much time as possible pushing my two children in the big pram away from the house. On one occasion the family dog Chum followed me. In spite of shouting at him to go back home he still followed so I just carried on pushing the pram down a country lane. I just passed the farm when Chum dashed up to me with a chicken in his jaws, followed by the farmer with a red rage. He raved at me about my so and so dog but when of I burst into tears and explained, he was very understanding.

Gladys Barratt

Approximately a half of the schools were sent to towns and villages in Kent; no nearer than places like Otford, Shoreham and Swanley, and extending out to Tonbridge, Tunbridge Wells, Ashford, Tenterden, and to the coast at Folkestone and Hythe. The remainder were split fairly evenly between east Surrey and east Sussex. Redhill, Reigate, Oxted, Horley and Bletchingly were prominent in receiving the schools which boarded trains at Sydenham, Forest Hill, Brockley and New Cross Gate stations. In Sussex, schools ended up in places as spread out as Battle, Lewes, Hove, Brighton, Bexhill, Hastings, Rye and Eastbourne. Only exceptionally was a local school sent in 1939 to a reception area outside the broad bounds indicated by these examples.

"BRING YOUR GASMASKS, THE PIGS SMELL"

How did they fare in their new surroundings? Were they happy? Were they well-treated? Did they pine for their families and old familiar neighbourhoods? According to early reports, everything in the Garden of England was lovely.

Local head teachers wrote to say, "All children are well and happy in this reception area. Everyone is doing his best to make the children feel at home. They are supervised by their foster parents and so are never out on their own. We are exceptionally favoured by brilliant sunshine so far...." The last bit was true, at any rate.

Sydenham children were reported to be in a "healthy part of Surrey" and were being well looked after. Brockley children were "very, very happy and fortunate". The story was the same from Tonbridge to Hastings - "Really happy, clean and tidy" and "hostesses had no criticisms of any sort". In Bexhill they were welcomed "with open arms", and at Ashford, the Mayor of Lewisham said, after visiting Catford and Downham children, that "they all looked very happy....and remarkably well."

For parents back home it was reassuring news, because it was not easy for them to find out for themselves - very few owned a car (petrol was rationed in any case) and the telephone was another rare possession. Reassurance was the name of the game. The expected air raids on London had not materialised, and the government was desperate that evacuees should not be enticed back. It would undo all the careful and

They hated us there

We was evacuated. We was only down there a month but they treated us terrible. They didn't like Londoners going there. My father signed up. He didn't have to go in but he signed up to go in. My mother wrote to him and said how bad it was so he went AWOL and come down and brought us home to London. Down at Tavistock. I was only four or five but I remember being down there. They hated us down there.

Richard White

They made me a domestic slave

My mother made me go away when my little girl was three months old because they had no-one looking after me and I wouldn't go in the shelters and she was worried about me. I went away for three months but I had a terrible life there so I brought them home and thought, "That's it, back to London". I went to South Wales. She was a farmer, a little wizened old lady, with a hump on her back. I was a slave there. My boy was a year and nine months old and the girl was three months old. In the morning I got up, there was no curtains on the window. I used to have to crawl along the floor because it looked right over the yard where they were bringing the

EVACUATION

THE GOVERNMENT HAVE DECIDED THAT IF THERE ARE AIR RAIDS YOU WILL HAVE ANOTHER CHANCE OF SENDING YOUR CHILDREN AWAY.

THIS TIME THE CHILDREN WILL NOT GO UNTIL AIR RAIDS MAKE IT NECESSARY.

THE NEW SCHEME WILL BE FOR SCHOOL CHILDREN WHO WERE AT SCHOOL LAST JULY, OR WHO HAVE REACHED THE AGE OF FIVE SINCE. IT APPLIES TO NO OTHERS.

NOW IS YOUR OPPORTUNITY TO REGISTER YOUR CHILDREN FOR EVACUATION. FILL UP THIS PAPER AND RETURN IT AT ONCE.

You are free to make up your mind, but you must MAKE UP YOUR MIND NOW. It is your duty to do so for the sake of your children. The authorities cannot make their plans at all if they do not know how many they have got to provide for.

If you want any help or there is anything you do not understand go to the nearest school, where you will either be able to get help or you will be told where you can.

HAPPY DEPTFORD CHILDREN.

costly planning which had gone into their dispersal; reduce education to a state of total chaos; and, not least, once more expose the children to bombing should it start.

Local newspapers were glad to report humour among the evacuees. If they could joke in their letters home, then things must be all right with them. A little New Cross girl wrote urging her mother to visit, adding, "Bring your gasmask, as the pigs smell". Another child wrote, with a nice reassuring touch, "We would like you to come and see how brown and freckled we're getting....We have a lovely bathing pool which is not deep enough to drown in."

"I GO, I COME BACK"

[Catch phrase of the character 'Ali Oop' in the radio show ITMA]

Just as the brilliant Indian summer of 1939 faded, so for many evacuees did the charms of country life away from their families - quite quickly in some cases. Slight jarring notes became detectable in the local papers. "The great majority of evacuees are happy, despite some tales to the contrary", said the Kentish Mercury. And again, "99 per cent are happy, but there are a few misfits".

For reasons that were many and diverse a steady stream began to return to London. As early as October the Mayor of Lewisham confessed to being "appalled by the numbers now seen playing about in the streets". By the end of the year "evacuation had broken down", according to the Lewisham Borough News, and thousands of idle children were "running wild" in the streets. Even the boys of St Dunstan's College had decided that evacuation was for weekdays only. They were reported cycling home at weekends from their billets in Reigate. However, the people for whom the whole thing had been a social disaster were the mothers who went with their pre-school infants. Their special needs simply could not be met in most homes without friction, and 90 per cent were back again by November. Some were back within 48 hours - like a Lee mother with

cows in for milking. I used to crawl along the floor, get in the corner and put my clothes on. Before I could have a cup of tea, I had to do all the housework, do the beds, clean the stairs down. Monday was her washday and that was about three hours with a dolly tub and sheets and all that.

They wouldn't do anything to help me at all. Why I come home - my two babies went lousy. The lice was about a quarter of an inch big. Imagine me sitting there all day at my kids' heads. My boy used to scream, "Mummy, please don't do it any more!" She used to sit out there with her fowls, plucking them, and you could see these damn things and it was making me ill worrying about me kids 'cause I was washing their hair and cutting it. She said, "It's only lice, it won't hurt them, for goodness sake, stop making a fuss". I said, "Well, I'm going home".

Flo Batley

They were lovely to us

They came round prior to September, the authorities, and said to my father, "Do you think the children should go to safety?" and he asked us and we went, "Yes, we'd like to go", thinking it would be fun.

five infants who were "not wanted" in Folkestone and spent the first night billeted in the local fever hospital. She wrote afterwards, "I have never been so glad to see my home....I would not leave my home again for anybody". The government never again attempted to find accommodation for this category of evacuees.

In March 1940 Londoners were again asked to register their children for evacuation, which would take place only if air raids started. Only 20 per cent bothered to reply and half of these wrote back simply to say that their children would stay in London whatever happened. The new registration scheme is a failure, the Kentish Independent declared: "It is unfortunate that London people do not give better support to the scheme....but it does show what they think of the war".

THE SECOND EXODUS - JUNE 1940

What Londoners thought of the war changed dramatically after Dunkirk, just two months later. The imminent threat of heavy air raids and the distinct possibility of invasion produced a sudden rush to register children for immediate evacuation. It took a week or two to organise the massive undertaking, but by 18 June 1940 many thousands of youngsters had left Deptford and Lewisham for destinations in the West Country. There was no place for them in Kent and Sussex, the coastal parts of which were themselves being evacuated westwards.

As in September 1939, evacuation parties assembled in school playgrounds, but this time schools did not travel as self-contained units - they scarcely existed as such, for some pupils and staff had not returned from the first evacuation, and some schools were still closed. Instead, the assembly points served children in the general area, including those who had been "running wild" since the previous autumn.

At the Elfrida Crescent assembly point over 500 proceeded to Catford station for trains travelling directly to Liskeard, as did a further 400 from Holbeach Road. Parties assembling at Mantle Road went to East Dulwich station for Paignton or to Honor Oak station for Crewkerne. And at Brockley Road they proceeded to Peckham Rye station for trains direct to Bideford.

On 3rd September 1939 we were evacuated. We got on a train that took us to Caterham in Surrey and then we got on a coach and we were all directed to our different coaches. Some went to Oxted or Limpsfield. We went to Tatsfield. We went from Brockley to Caterham, from Caterham to Tatsfield by coach.

The first people they took us to were very poor. I think they were given 7/6d a week for our keep. There was Joan, Sheila and me, all sisters. When we got there it was such a poor house that the billeting officer said, "I can't let them stay here. It is quite obvious to me you can't have them." Well, the woman looked a bit ill herself, and her children looked a bit thin and pale. So the billeting lady took us to her house which was called Crayford Cottage. She had a maid called Dorothy. They were lovely to us. But she obviously was a Miss and she wasn't really used to children. She didn't have a lot of idea of motherhood, but she was very kind. My parents came and visited us and brought sacks of potatoes down to her. Like taking coals to Newcastle! They came to visit us to ask us how we were. We were saying, "It's lovely."

Pat McDonald

THEY WERE ONLY ASKING

[How one local parent responded to the 1940 registration form}

PARENT'S NAME:
Not so blind.

HOME ADDRESS:
Happy Christian, London.

CHILDREN'S NAMES:
Ye serpents of a Generation of Vipers, fight your own battles. It's to your interest, not mine. My children will not leave to serve Satan if I can help it.

(Item quoted from official evacuation files in the GLC Archives)

Compared with the first evacuation, little public interest was shown in how this new wave of refugees coped among strange surroundings. Evacuation was no longer the novelty it had been. More to the point, the people had more urgent matters to think about. The Battle of Britain was getting into its stride and the Blitz would soon follow. No one wished to hear tearful stories from evacuees sorry for themselves. The war, which had been vicious and ruthless at sea from the beginning, had suddenly become a serious business for everyone. Evacuees could consider themselves lucky and well out of it.

"Don't be a kid or a weeping willow", ran the line in the song **'Goodnight Children, Everywhere'.**

LEAVING UNDER BATTLE CONDITIONS

When the London Blitz began in September 1940 an evacuation system 'on tap' was already in place. This was designed particularly for children (and certain adults) who lost their homes in the bombing, but also for any parent who had second thoughts about sending their children to a safer place. It is not possible to generalise about this on-going movement, yet it differed from the others in one major respect - most of the evacuees departed under actual battle conditions. Journeys (usually by bus) to London rail termini were constantly interrupted by air raid sirens, the sound of gunfire, and danger from falling bombs.

Counties in south-west England continued to receive most of those who left Deptford and Lewisham under what was called the 'trickle' evacuation scheme. Some also left for South Wales and other parts of the kingdom. Astonishing though it seemed to people in official places, something greater than a trickle of evacuees began returning to London, even while the Blitz raged. By November 1940 the number returning actually exceeded the outflow.

A CLASH OF CULTURES

Returning home from evacuation, a London boy had clearly been subjected to middle class ideas of politeness. When his mother opened the door, he raised his cap and greeted her with the words, **"Good afternoon, Mother"**. She replied, **"Don't you talk to me like that, else I'll give you a clip round the ear 'ole"**.

Foster mother was a prostitute

In the end four children went to Northampton. One of them, Grace, went to the village prostitute and she said she was the kindest person she'd ever met. She told me no-one would speak to this woman, and the lady Margaret was with wouldn't allow Margaret to visit her there. Gracy could come to see them but Margaret mustn't go to see Grace. Grace said to me, "What is a prostitute Mum? My foster mother is a prostitute and she is a very nice woman." She never interfered with the kids or me either, so that was it. George went to another place with a very old couple. We still keep in touch with the children as they have grown up. Bessy went to Northampton fire station to the chief of the Fire Brigade. They were very nice people.

Mrs Darling

I wouldn't go away again

I was evacuated to Exmouth in Devon when I was about nine or ten. I didn't see my mother or father for a whole year because my father was in the airforce, and my mother wouldn't come down unless my father got leave, and anyway Devon was such a long way to come. I used to write of course, but all I ever said was, "Send money" or "Send sweets". I also kept

THE FLIGHT FROM 'BUZZ BOMB ALLEY'

If some evacuees insisted on returning to London while the Blitz was in progress, it was only to be expected that a lot more would return when the Blitz ended. Which is what they did. Whereas the population of Deptford and Lewisham stood at only 65 per cent of its pre-war total during the 1940 bombing, it had risen again to 85-90 per cent by 1942, a year after the last raids of the Blitz.

Enough children were back by 1942 to justify the full-time re-opening of schools, those which were still standing. Extensive first-aid repairs might be needed on many of the others, but there was no shortage of pupils to fill them. When air raids resumed in 1943 and early 1944 they appeared to make little difference either way to the desire of people to stay in the capital. The schools continued to operate without interruption.

But the arrival, by day and night, of the malevolent VI flying bombs, or Doodlebugs, in June 1944 brought an immediate suspension of lessons throughout south east London. No doubt they would have triggered large-scale evacuation immediately, too, only it was not until three weeks later that a government-organised scheme was started. This time it was entirely up to individual families to put their names down and await their turn. Schools played no part in it, except that those which were originally evacuated to places now in 'buzz bomb alley', and remained together there, found themselves uprooted a second time. Such schools included Colfe's, sent from Tunbridge Wells to Frome; Aske's, removed from Oxted to Teignmouth; and St Dunstan's, sent from Reigate to Caerphilly (no cycling home from there).

307,000 mothers and children left London under the official scheme, which lasted from 5 July until 7 September 1944, plus a further 552,000 who went off privately or accepted 'billeting tickets and free travel vouchers'. They went away to Wales, to the Midlands, to the north....anywhere so long as it was not south.

asking to be allowed to come home. I'd wanted to go in the first place because it was an adventure, but then the gilt had worn off the gingerbread and I wanted to go back. My mother wouldn't let me because the Blitz was at its height. At last my father came down to see me on his own. By this time I think they had bombed Exmouth itself and I said I didn't want to stay. I think he must have given me some money because I can remember sending my mother a telegram saying, "Meet me at Waterloo." She was furious, but I came home and wouldn't go away again.

Jean Carter

Evacuees from Athelney Street School, Bellingham at Shoreham, Kent. (C.W.Barnett).

HOME FOR GOOD

When the flying bombs effectively ceased their carnage, their place was taken by the sinister V2 long-range rockets. This should have been enough to induce the evacuees to stay put, but true to past form they began to pour back to London regardless of the danger. Even Winston Churchill felt bound to say that "while a daring and adventurous spirit was to be commended, this needless risk and movement should be discouraged".

Back they came, all the same. Schools re-opened in Deptford and Lewisham yet again, ignoring the extra-mural thunder-crashes of Hitler's latest vengeance weapons. When Londoners were at last officially told they could return home, instead of trains for an expected half-million being required, there were just 50,000 mothers and children wanting transport. For those who stuck out evacuation since the early days homecoming often turned out to be more traumatic than the original separation.

Travelling in wartime in the **blackout** was rather difficult, to say the least. Signposts were **blacked** out, as were names on stations. The **blackout** confused everybody, friend as well as the expected foe. Trains were dimly lit with blue lighting and the blinds were kept down once it was dark, so it was very difficult to recognise one station from another, even on familiar journeys.

Edie McHardy

Having been re-evacuated from the south coast in June 1940, boys from Stanley Street School, Deptford take a morning dip in a Pembrokeshire lake.

Put that b....y light out!

This was the well-known yell, according to popular belief, of an officious air raid warden, directed at some unfortunate miscreant breaking the Black Out rules.

The offender might be a householder who had left a chink of light showing through a gap in the heavy Black Out curtains. It might be a pedestrian waving his No. 8 torchlight in the air, instead of keeping it pointed towards the ground. It might be a smoker failing to shield a lighted match in his cupped hand....

Whoever it was and whatever his supposed misdeed, his hackles were sure to be raised by the crude command. The Black Out was the leading grievance in the early months of the war. Being shouted at like a raw recruit on the parade ground did not improve tempers. But you didn't argue with the man, or tell him where he could go....Otherwise a policeman or two would join the party and you might find yourself appearing before the Greenwich magistrates.

A Catford man was fined £2 for showing a light, which he said was so dim that the policeman bringing the prosecution had borrowed his torch so he could see to write down the particulars.

A Forest Hill man was fined £3 (call it £100 in today's money) for "wilfully displaying a torchlight" and assaulting the police officer who ordered him to put it out.

"When the warden called about a light showing in the house, the man told him he was 'a sponger on the rates' and 'ought to be in the trenches', then knocked him to the ground." (Kentish Mercury report)

In Lewisham the residents had gone out leaving a light showing in an upper window. A crowd of people gathered to watch and applaud when a policeman, armed with a brush and a pot of paint, climbed a ladder and painted out the window in black. (Lewisham Borough News)

UNTIL YOUR EYES GET USED TO THE DARKNESS, TAKE IT EASY

LOOK OUT IN THE BLACKOUT

HE THOUGHT HE COULD JUST DO IT

WATCH OUT IN THE BLACK OUT!

Britain's Black Out regulations came into force on Friday, 1 September 1939 - two days before we declared war - and lasted with some modifications until April 1945. They were extremely strict and rigorously enforced. There were no street lights. No lights in shop windows after about 6pm. Car headlamps had to be covered by metal masks with just three narrow, hooded slits allowing a small patch of light to seep out. Traffic lights were heavily shielded and almost entirely blotted out.

'Doing the black out' was a nightly chore for every household. "It takes me quite half an hour every night", one woman told the Mass Observation researchers at Blackheath. Chintz and other light fabrics would not do. It was a case of heavy, thick curtains, tightly drawn. Or blankets, even carpets, pinned up. Many people fitted wooden shutters outside the windows to make absolutely sure no glimmer of light escaped.

THEY JOKED ABOUT IT - BUT IT WAS NO JOKE

In the winter of 1939-1940 more people were being killed in road accidents due to the Black Out than on active service in all the armed forces combined.

"Our streets are almost as dangerous as the battlefield," said the Kentish Mercury editorial. If they meant the battlefield in France, then only 15 British soldiers were killed there to the end of 1939, against 3,000 deaths on the roads at home. Meanwhile, how many civilians had been killed in air raids? The answer, as a contemporary report acidly said, was "one Scotch rabbit" - a reference to a rabbit killed by an enemy bomb in the Shetlands in November 1939.

Danger lay not only in our streets. Hazards lay in wait for the unwary at every turn. "On dark nights it is really a matter of groping one's way with nerves as well as hands held out into the future of the next moment," Mass Observation was told.

- A Downham man fell off Shortlands station platform into the street below and was killed.

- A youth was injured when he fell down the embankment of Catford station.

- A Lewisham man fell into the Surrey Docks and drowned.

- Another died after falling into an open trench air raid shelter.

- Every kerbside, every tree and lamp-post, every piece of uneven pavement, a carelessly left bicycle....They brought a catalogue of broken or sprained ankles, bruised heads, cracked shins....

- Bumping into other pedestrians, too, was known to lead to falls that could prove fatal.

PULL THE OTHER ONE:

A local pensioner well-known to the police for his partiality to the bottle appeared before Greenwich magistrates for the 230th time on a charge of being drunk and incapable. His excuse this time was that he could not see in the Black Out "so lay down on the pavement to get out of danger."!

Overheard: "This Black Out's going to cause a lot of trouble. I asked if I could see her home before I realised I'd bumped into my wife."

There were compensations, though. On a clear night London's skies once more became beautifully star-lit to the naked eye. Or under the cool beams of a full moon the empty streets glistened like silver in an almost rural atmosphere of calm and tranquillity. It was said that London reverted to a collection of small villages in the war. The Black Out had a lot to do with that, for it deterred people from travelling far from their homes.

Bless 'em All

Some volunteered, but most waited their turn to be called up. No point in meeting trouble half way, unless one felt the urge of duty strongly or was hoping to cut a heroic figure among friends and neighbours. Volunteering for military service might be all right for a young man without family responsibilities, but in a married man such haste to serve one's country could look suspiciously like an excuse to leave the wife.

The call-up process started with registration at the local Labour Exchange on a date determined by your age and the initial letter of your surname. This was your chance to specify which branch of the services you would like to join, or to apply for exemption or even as a conscientious objector. By mid-1941 all men aged between $18\frac{1}{2}$ and 41 had registered, including some 35,000 from Deptford and Lewisham.

Then came the medical a few weeks later. The war-time army medical was the source of much humour. The general impression put about was that if you were breathing, then you were AI fit. Shortly afterwards the call-up papers arrived, including a rail pass, informing you of which branch of the services you had been allocated to, your service number, and where and when you were to report for basic training. About 14 days notice was given in order to give time to prepare for the coming trauma of separation from civilian life. Then abruptly and without further formality the gates of your old life clanged shut behind you. You were now subject to military law and discipline, and could choose to make the best of it or suffer the consequences of trying to fight the system.

It took about three months to knock the civilian stuffing out of a raw recruit and turn him into something resembling a soldier (or sailor or airman). Blood, sweat and tears ... the training almost always worked.

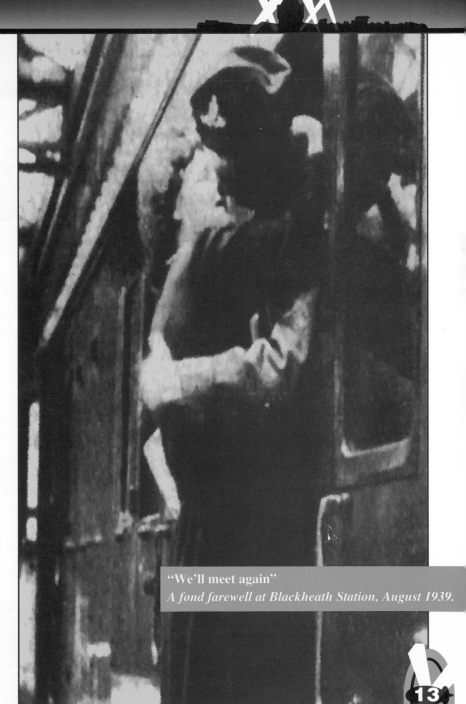

"We'll meet again"
A fond farewell at Blackheath Station, August 1939.

Meanwhile, popular songs offered a little light relief and consolation for the poor recruit's predicament:

Bless 'em all, the long and the short and the tall...

Kiss me goodnight, sergeant-major; sergeant-major be a mother to me...

Ma, I miss your apple pie; Ma, I miss your stew...

Our sergeant-major, his medals break our hearts, he won them playing darts...

It was what happened after training that really mattered. The luck of the draw would determine whether you were in the wrong place at the wrong time. Whether, that is, you were killed or wounded or captured in an overseas war-zone, or, for example, spent the whole time in a remote, rain-soaked posting somewhere in the farthest reaches of the British Isles.

Naval ratings and paratroops of the Airborne Regiment in Deptford for 'Wings for Victory' week.

Call Up - Reminiscences

I was exempt from the war as I was an agricultural worker. I had a different stamp card from the ordinary one. I had a brown one. I wish I hadn't have gone. I'm suffering for it, for my silly mistake. I went because my mates went. That's all it was for everyone. Your mates went, you went. Immaterial if you were exempt or not.

Blown up at Crete

I done quite a bit of fighting and I seen all the killing and murdering. Then I got blown up in a naval ship, coming away from Crete. On that boat, they took the ones that were alive off it to Alexandria and the rest they took down to South Africa to bury them down there. We got word two or three months after that there was just under 600 dead on that boat the Cruiser Ryan.

I got all my bones broken. I laid in that hospital in the marquee, in a case from my neck right the way down on the right hand. I laid there God knows how long - it must have been getting on for a year, I think. I was never any good after that.

Paralysed and reported dead

When I got blown up on the ship, it blew all my clothes off and I lost my tags. They didn't know who I was because I couldn't speak or move my hands or anything. I was paralysed. Couldn't say anything. So the War Office were very kind - they sent my death certificate to her and said she would receive a pension. I wasn't dead.My wife was on the trams in London during the war. Anyway, her driver on the tram, he was very upset. He went to the War Office and they couldn't have cared less. Wasn't interested. They tried to find out if I was alive or dead first. So he said, "Come on Edith, we'll go to the Red Cross". That was up at Hyde Park Corner. They said "Come back in three days time and we'll tell you." And they told her that I was in hospital, where I was and everything. And then she went to the War Office again. They said "We don't take notice of somebody else." That's part of the Government, isn't it? They are callous, for what you've done. I'm good for nothing, can't hardly get about. I can't go out unless I'm in a battery chair. After what I've seen. I'm very sorry I took that action because I lost a good job and good money fighting for this country.

Mr Harper

One that nearly got away

There's a little story attached to my husband, bless him. We got married on Easter Saturday. But he had his calling up papers on the Wednesday and he said, "No chance." He didn't go in the army and he was on the run for two and a half years. He had to live on his wits because he had no pass. He used to have to take any old job, for nothing, do up old vans, or he'd be down the fish market or somewhere like that. We always let ourselves go, did without, as long as the kids had biscuits or something. It was a struggle. It was more harder for him being out of the army than not. He was on the run for two and a half years and I think he got shopped at the end.

Flo Batley

Local TA units of the Royal Engineers at camp in the New Forest, Hampshire, 1939.

The First 'Casualty' - Education

It was said at the time that education was the first casualty of the war. London education was certain to become a casualty in due course. That it became so immediately was due not to enemy action, but to the agreed necessity of evacuating school children from high-risk areas before enemy action forced it upon the capital. Also a victim of the crisis was the raising of the school-leaving age from 14 to 15, which had been due to come into effect on 1 September 1939. This was postponed 'for the duration of the emergency', only coming into effect finally in the summer of 1945.

Once the schools had been vacated by their staff and pupils they were immediately occupied by the ARP services, the Auxiliary Fire Service, and other organisations connected with the defence of London. It did not prove easy to get them out again when the unexpected drift back of evacuees led to a demand for the schools to be re-opened.

For those Deptford and Lewisham children who stayed at home in September 1939 there was virtually no schooling available at all, although a system of visiting tutors to pupils' homes or in hired premises for an hour or two a week came into operation. For the evacuees in reception areas it was a case of 'doubling up' with local schools or in church halls on a part-time basis.

The flow of returning evacuees produced complete disarray in London's educational system. By November there were as many children back in the capital as there were in the reception areas. Local schools and their teachers were scattered all over Kent, Surrey and Sussex while the pupils vanished into thin air. The staff were in one place and most of the children were somewhere else.

Back home the schools remained closed - and for three good reasons. First, there were no teachers to staff them. Second, they lacked air raid shelters. And, third, the Civil Defence organisations would not budge. There was another reason - the authorities did not want the children there. Re-opening the schools would only encourage more back.

The village school in rural Somerset attended by the author, Lewis Blake, as an evacuee, in 1941

Examples of part-time sharing in 1939

Blackheath High School with *Tunbridge Wells High School*

Honor Oak County Girls' with *Reigate County Girls'*

Colfe's with *The Skinner's School, Tunbridge Wells*

Haberdasher Aske's Boys with *Oxted County School*

Prendergast with *Tonbridge County School for Girls*

St Dunstan's with *Reigate Grammar School*

SE London Technical with *Loughborough Technical College*

Sydenham County Girls' with *Dorking County Girls'*

Sydenham High School with *Brighton High School*

Colfe's School, Lewisham at Tunbridge Wells, where they shared with the Skinner's School.

PART-TIME SCHOOLING FOR SOME

Things could not go on like this. Everyone was complaining that "kids were running wild in the streets." After considerable efforts involving the ejection of some Civil Defence units, the building of splinter proof walls outside classroom windows, and the recall of about 1,000 teachers, a system of part-time schooling was introduced in January 1940 on a voluntary basis for 11 to 14-year-olds only. Later it became compulsory in places where it was available, and was extended to some other age-groups.

Called the 'emergency school system', it started off with only 78 schools in the whole of London. Those in Lewisham included St Michael's and St Bartholomew's, Sydenham; Ballamore Road and Durham Hill, Downham; and Rathfern Road and Plassy Road, Catford. Single-storey school premises on the LCC estates, such as Elfrida Crescent and Athelney Street, never did qualify for the scheme because they lacked adequate overhead protection from bullets and splinters.

The second large-scale evacuation in June 1940, followed by the London blitz in the autumn and winter, completely undermined the emergency school system just as it was beginning to reach the majority of local children. Even before the bombing started, part of Lewisham's and Deptford's school population were dispersed all over the West Country. Others were still with what remained of their schools in Kent, Surrey and Sussex. Some of these, however, had been re-evacuated from exposed coastal areas to Wales and elsewhere. While yet another sizeable group stuck it out at home with little prospect of being taught at all.

Frequent daylight air raids during the autumn of 1940 made school attendance in south east London largely pointless, even if the resources had been there to cater for non-evacuated children. Added to which the heavy nightly bombing took a steady toll on school premises:

Sandhurst Road, Elfrida Crescent, St Stephen's, Durham Hill, Monson Road, Aske's Boys and Aske's Girls, Rathfern Road, Churchdown, and Forest Hill Central were some of the schools substantially damaged by fire or blast in the opening phase of the blitz.

A striking picture of schoolboys filing down the school staircase in a shelter drill, wearing their gasmasks. (October 1941).

SCHOOLING MADE COMPULSORY AGAIN

Come what may, the school and health authorities were determined to get non-evacuated London children off the streets and into some kind of schooling. There were probably some 6,000-7,000 in this category in Deptford and Lewisham at the height of the bombing. Wherever it could be provided, education was made compulsory for all elementary school children from December 1940. Being made to return to the classroom was a painful experience for the youth of the district.

The middle years of the war, from 1942 to mid-1944, turned out to be the most settled period for children's education, relatively speaking. But it was of a very basic 'make-do-and-mend' kind. Many teachers were, in the words of a war-time song, "either too young or too old". Actually, the pupils probably benefited from having past-retirement teachers and middle-aged mothers who had been recalled to the profession. The job called for lots of experience and the children needed a steady, mature hand.

This meant, however, there was seldom anyone to take games, swimming, or physical exercise. Not that visits to playing fields, swimming baths, or indeed anywhere else off the school premises would have been permitted, unless air raid shelters were available. A temporary easing of this restriction came about in May 1942, allowing Deptford, for example, to recommence swimming lessons at Laurie Grove.

It was all a matter of pot-luck as to what the children received beyond the basic 3-Rs. If there just happened to be a music teacher on the staff, then they got singing lessons. If there happened to be a woodwork room and a teacher willing to supervise it, then the boys might get the chance of developing some skill at carpentry. At Haseltine Road, Sydenham, however, woodwork lessons were conducted without the benefit of wood! Such was the nature of war-time shortages.

The arrival of V1 flying bombs in June 1944 put paid even to this 'utility' brand of education, heralding yet another period of total disruption. Not until the late-autumn, with the thundering V2 rockets coming down without warning, did local schools start picking up the pieces again. The rockets were simply ignored. You couldn't shelter from them, so non-evacuated children were in no greater danger at school than in their homes.

Out of this mess London education somehow contrived to extricate itself and plan for the return of peace-time conditions. Yet a whole generation of Londoners were to carry with them for the rest of their lives the scars of a ruined and ramshackle war-time education.

Local schools were occupied by units of the Civil Defence from the beginning of the war. Here AFS motor cyclists are seen at their sub-station in Adamsrill Road School, Sydenham.

Fair Shares For All

Food rationing was introduced in January 1940, covering at first sugar, butter and bacon, then meat. But you could not walk into just any grocer or butcher to buy your weekly portions.

First you had to be registered with a particular retailer of your choice, for better or worse. And that meant a trip to the local Food Control Office, armed with your ration book and your Identity Card. There it was like a doctor's surgery - lots of people in front of you waiting their turn. In normal circumstances you might change your retailer only once a year when ration books were renewed, unless you moved house meanwhile, or something of that kind.

Those 1940 ration books contained plenty of pages for the introduction of further foodstuffs to the scheme. In July, tea (2oz per week), margarine or butter (6oz per week), and lard (2oz per week) were added. 1941 saw cheese (1oz-2oz), jam, marmalade, syrup (8oz-2lb per month), and milk 2-2½ pints per week) included. Two eggs a month was fairly standard, but more during the laying season around Easter-time.

By 1942 sweets and chocolate had joined the list (½lb-1lb per month), as had soap (3oz-4oz per month). The ingenious 'points' system came into operation in 1941. A whole range of non-basic foodstuffs were given certain points ratings, and each ration-book contained so many points per month which could be used on these products. At first each person was allocated 32 points, later reduced to 24 per month. Most tinned foods, cereals, biscuits, and so on were covered, but it was not necessary to register with a retailer when using one's points.

In 1942, a 1lb tin of stewed steak or red salmon rated 32 points - a whole month's allocation for one person. You did better with a 1lb tin of pilchards, only 12 points, or better still with a small tin of sardines, just 4 points. 1942 witnessed the introduction of tinned dried milk and

Going Bananas at the Greengrocers

There wasn't any rationing of vegetables. Bananas were rationed for children. A child under five had a green ration book and that entitled them to have bananas when you had them. But you didn't go to the market and buy them. You had a card sent from the Ministry of Food saying you were entitled to boxes of bananas. Then you'd go and take this card and get them. When you brought them, all hell would break loose. People would hear, "They've got bananas" and come - they would have killed you for it.

I used to think to myself, "If it was peacetime they wouldn't buy any bananas. You could have thousands and nobody'd buy them". But because there was a shortage, everybody wanted them. I had experience from my father before the war when I used to go out. He used to say, "Say I've got bananas. I want to get rid of them. They'll be going off by the weekend." I'd say, "Would you like four nice bananas?" to them. I suppose they thought I was precocious. If I didn't sell them my Dad would say, "I don't want to sell potatoes. They won't go off. Make them have bananas." He used to sell them on the rounds up Catford and Brockley. He had regular

the arrival from the USA of tinned Spam and boxes of dried egg. A 4oz box of dried egg contained the equivalent of twelve eggs and, like Spam, you had to give up some of your points for it.

Austerity Christmas party for the infants of Childeric Road School, New Cross, 1943. A fresh apple was a treat, but they were too young to remember what an orange was like.

SOME FOODS WERE NOT RATIONED

The National Wholemeal Loaf was introduced to save on imported wheat. It also helped to save the nation from bread and flour rationing in the war years, as well as being more healthy than white bread. It was not enough, however, to prevent a period of bread rationing <u>after</u> the war.

'Potato Pete' was a Ministry of Food propaganda figure that exhorted everyone to eat more potatoes and less bread. The famous 'Woolton Pie' - named after Lord Woolton, Minister of Food - was one of many vegetable recipes urged on a reluctant population. In it potatoes figured prominently. The home-grown spud remained un-rationed throughout, providing the nation's diet with much of what it needed of bulk, if not of variety.

Fish and chips continued as a staple meal for great numbers of working people, though there was usually quite a scrum to face in the fish shop. Somehow supplies held out without the assistance of rationing, despite a reduced fishing fleet and the dangers fishermen faced at sea. The humble sausage also escaped the net of rationing. No one liked to enquire into what it contained. Whatever it was, sausages were in short supply and housewives usually had to join long queues to get their share. It was a common sight for queues to form outside the branches of a popular south east London purveyor of sausages long before the shops were due to open for business.

rounds. When the war came, and directly they knew - Mrs Brown would go to Mrs Green and say, "Look I've got bananas." They'd come flying down. "Bananas!" I'd say, "Sorry, they've gone." "Yeah. There won't always be a war on." I'd say, "There will while you're alive!"

Pat McDonald

The kids ate beetroot sandwiches

Rations was very painful. You got eight penny worth of meat, but our butcher used to make us stuff called sausage savoury. I think it was stuffing but you would buy it by the pound and you would put it between pieces of pastry and the kids ate it. It was called sausage savoury, I don't think I ever saw a sausage, I am sure I didn't. That was at Dewhurst, that was sixpence a pound, and you got a pound and a half of that, that made a good dinner. And the children, if they were home and you wanted to give them something for their tea, you would give them beetroot sandwiches. You would pay a shilling for a beetroot which was a lot of money. They had to have beetroot sandwiches because it was good for them. We bought them raw. You bought a big beetroot for a shilling and then you cooked it and that had to do with bread and marge or whatever was for their tea.

Imported fresh fruit had become but a fond memory by about 1942. Small children had no memories at all of what it was to eat a banana or an orange. Such tropical exotica existed in the imagination but were hardly ever seen in the flesh.

UNDER THE COUNTER

Many manufactured goods inevitably became scarce, for supplies were restricted to one-third or less of pre-war levels. Early casualties of the Black Out were curtain materials and No. 8 torchlight batteries, the standard size at the time. Shortages of popular goods, such as cigarettes, produced the 'Under The Counter' syndrome. What it meant was that shopkeepers kept their supplies back for regular customers or for friends and favourites. It was a kind of reward for customer loyalty. The casual passer-by who dropped in to ask hopefully, "Do you have any cigarettes, please?", received a polite but stony answer in the negative, which he didn't believe but couldn't do much about.

Retailers received only small set quotas of almost anything one might care to name - pens, razor blades, toilet paper, matches, writing pads.... Some goods were not only hard to find; one also needed a special permit to buy them, as for typewriters and alarm clocks.

When petrol was rationed in 1939, the answer for Chiesman's Department Store in Lewisham was to go back to horse-drawn delivery vans.

The local Press regularly commented on the state of trade in Lewisham.

● **January 1940:**
No shortages of food were in evidence over Christmas.... Plenty of good cheer everywhere.... There are no food queues locally, not like 1917.... The winter sales are in full swing, with many bargains. But shortages of clothes, shoes and fabrics are bound to appear....

● **Summer 1941:**
More commodities are becoming scarce, like cleaning, washing, and toilet preparations.... Shops are closing through lack of supplies.... Tinned fruit has virtually disappeared.... Furniture and toy dealers are suffering from lack of goods.... Queueing is now noticed to be spreading as the established way of doing business. Some queues at Lewisham and Catford street markets are quite unnecessary.

But you couldn't always get your rations, that was another thing. I used to walk miles and miles to get a pig's trotter, things like that, I would walk to Deptford to get pigs' trotters. One day I had to do some work, had no money and I walked to Crofton Park in Brockley and I pushed three kids in a pram to do a morning's work and back again. But you didn't think, we did things like that in those days.

We were so poor that we didn't have any money, but there was one thing that we did not do: we didn't buy or sell a coupon. My husband and I felt very strongly about it: it was against our principles.

Mrs Darling

Save all tapes, ribbons, pieces of elastic, hooks, eyes, press fastenings, buttons and trimmings from old clothes.

Use soft water or rain-water wherever possible to save soap.

Rinse stockings in warm water after each wearing.

You should use your precious soap for washing them only when they are dirty.

You can wash them after your bath in the same water, using soap for the soles only.

Turning Grown-up's Discarded Garments Into Children's Clothes

Grey flannel trousers will make boys' shorts and girls' skirts.

Pygama legs will make children's vests.

Old woollen stockings can be made into a child's jersey.

UTILITY MAKES ITS MARK

Clothes rationing was introduced in June 1941 on its own points system. An unofficial trade in clothes coupons developed between those who needed money more than clothes and those with the cash to buy extra coupons. It was like stealing the clothes off another's back, yet so many poor people had gone about in rags in peace-time that it couldn't be said much had changed.

The accent was on serviceability and durability. Not the stuff of fashions. Women would not be seen in public without a hat in the old days, but now many went hatless or they wore headscarves. And they took to slacks, something no fashion-conscious woman would have been seen dead in once. What was the world coming to? 'Utility' clothes made to economy standards set by the government and sold at fixed prices took over. They were reasonably well-received, surprisingly. So perhaps women were secretly glad to be released from the tyranny of fashions.

Utility was everywhere - from furniture down to pencils. The manufacture of furniture was banned in 1942, except for 22 essential items on a points rationing system. The stuff was regarded as cheap and ugly-looking. Fifty years after the war they now say it is becoming collectable.

● What did a utility pencil look like? It was a plain piece of wood, unpainted and unsharpened. You used it until it was worn down to a stub.

● Cups were no longer cups; they were thick, plain white mugs without handles. Saucers you could do without - after all, it was 'common' to drink your tea out of one.

● Sweets were not wrapped. Biscuits were always sold loose, and there were only 20 varieties, compared to 350 pre-war. There was no silver paper around chocolate bars; in fact, the ends of the bar were not wrapped at all.

Nobody went hungry

Things as you know were rationed but in my opinion nobody ever went hungry or starving. The rations were small, but I believe they were quite adequate. The trouble as far as shopkeeping was concerned, was that when there was a bad period of the war, and we had a lot of raids, the people evacuated, but their provisions were still being delivered to the shop. So you had a lot more in the shop than you needed to have. There'd be another change in the war again, the raids would get bad and everybody would go away again, then the food office would cut your supplies down again. Then it would be quiet again and everybody would come back and you would be desperately short of food to make it all go around, because the farmers were running out of stuff and wouldn't be able to supply them with their rations. You were either plenty or short.

Mr Drury snr

The Butcher Rationed Sausages

The boss never had enough sausages or liver to supply everybody. They was off the rations you see, so of course you formed your own rationing system by putting a mark on their ration books and saying, "Bring your ration books with you," and saying, "You had sausages last week. You can't have them this week." They settled down to it. The mornings when they knew we were going to have sausages in, they would queue outside the shop before we opened in the morning. They knew what days the deliveries were. They knew what merchant would call on that particular day so they were all there.

Eggs were another thing that weren't rationed really. You weren't supplied,

so we had to mark the books with those. We weren't short of eggs because my wife's father kept chickens so we had extra from them all the time.

I looked after myself, you wouldn't believe me if I said I didn't. I do know places that had branch managers who were very strict on their staff and wouldn't allow them to have any extra at all. But we did have a little bit extra, those that worked in the shop did. Yes. Because there were times when you had so much stuff in the shop, so plentiful, as I told you. And then all of a sudden it would be completely the other way.

Mr Drury snr

Queued Hours For Tomatoes

It's funny because as soon as we heard any of the shops had anything in, my mother used to say, "Go on Daisy, you run up and get in the line." And all these children were trying to get in the line where they could. If anyone had any tomatoes going, ooh God my husband used to go everywhere to try and get tomatoes. When I was expecting Maggie we were kept in London, but some mothers were taken out of London, most of them were, and I had Maggie in the old Surrey Hall in Godalming, and it was strange 'cause my husband

was still in London after the war and every time he came down here, he used to try and get hold of some tomatoes, and if he knew some were going he would queue hours to try and get them to bring down to us.

Daisy Cook

Queues A Mile Long

Lewisham market kept reasonably solvent during the war until the V1s came along but obviously with the evacuation of the population and what have you it really became very sparse for the market to survive, though a few of the old traders did continue.

The rationing affected us the same as it did everyone else. You know, where goods were concerned we had an allocation of so many bananas when the boys managed to bring them across, so many oranges and what have you. There were not many imports like that, because the whole of the shipping was devoted to the war effort, but the occasional one got through. Well then of course they were a complete rarity in those days. The young children they hadn't even seen a banana. When they were offered for sale there used to be queues a mile long. It is one of those things you tell the younger generation about because it's very hard for them to realise how acute the shortages

IS **YOUR** GARDEN ON WAR SERVICE?

'DIG FOR VICTORY'

"Let 'Dig for Victory' be the motto for everyone with a garden."- Ministry of Agriculture message, 4 October 1939.

Lawns and flower beds, the pride and joy of suburbia, became slightly suspect as not helpful to the war effort when the 'Dig for Victory' campaign got going. It was cabbages the country needed, not chrysanthemums. Those without gardens could also join in the patriotic spadework by taking on a vegetable allotment. The number of allotments rose by 500,000 thereby adding 200,000 tons of fresh food annually to British larders.

By the summer of 1940 Lewisham Council had provided 2,450 additional plots covering 73 acres, mostly in public parks. Eventually this total rose above 3,000, and included five acres ploughed up for potatoes in Beckenham Place Park, while sheep grazed safely on the links in the absence of golfers.

Deptford, which experienced difficulty in providing allotments owing to a scarcity of open spaces, announced in 1940 that the keeping of pigs, poultry and rabbits on council estates was now permitted by government order. Soon chicken-runs and rabbit hutches sprouted in back gardens over town and suburb, adding a useful supplement of fresh meat and eggs to the diet of numerous families. Pigs were a different matter. Not very many householders felt up to keeping one. An extension of the 'waste not - want not' philosophy offered an alternative way of helping to fatten pigs. This involved the siting of pig-swill bins on street corners, into which food waste could be deposited: potato peelings, cabbage leaves, plate scrapings, and other kitchen delicacies guaranteed to attract flies and bluebottles in warm weather.

were. You might get an allocation of perhaps five boxes of tomatoes (because a few English growers who had not gone into the army were carrying on) and then you'd have to try and match them out by half a pound per person and all that sort of thing. Oh it was quite a performance really. If some of the imports did get here from South Africa or somewhere like that, like grapefruit or something which was a real rarity, of course that was a real bonus.

Mr Davis (market trader)

MAKE-DO AND MEND says Mrs. Sew-and-Sew

ISSUED BY THE BOARD OF TRADE

Dad's Call To Arms

"We want large numbers of men, aged 17-65, to offer their services to a force to be named 'The Local Defence Volunteers'"

(radio broadcast by Sir Anthony Eden, 14 May 1940)

The
HOME GUARD
POCKET MANUAL

Local Home Guard going through the 'gas van' in Deptford.

These words from the Secretary of State for War called upon men not already in uniform to join a force to fight, in the event of invasion, enemy paratroops dropped behind British lines. The force was later re-named the Home Guard - 'Dad's Army', as a popular television series many years after the war dubbed it.

Police stations throughout Deptford and Lewisham reported a steady stream of volunteers responding to Anthony Eden's appeal. Something like 25 enrolments an hour were recorded at Lee Green police station, many of whom were First World War and Boer War campaigners. One 64-year-old veteran said, "As long as I kill ten Germans, I don't care if I die."

The popular image of the Home Guard practising with nothing more lethal than pitchforks and broomsticks refers to a short initial period. From quite early on the 19th County of London Battalion (South Suburban Gas Company) trained regularly in rifle shooting, bayonet fighting, and grenade throwing. Ranges at Sydenham and Penfold's sand-pit, Lewisham were used for .22 rifle practice, while .303 shooting was conducted at Shoreham, Kent and Scadbury Park, Chislehurst. Other ranges catered for live grenade and bombing practice. Un-armed combat and silent killing methods received much attention, since the Home Guard was also viewed as a guerrilla warfare force.

Other battalions in the area included the 20th and 57th covering Lewisham, Catford and Beckenham; the 18th at Dulwich; and the 55th and 51st County of Kent battalions at Bromley and Beckenham.

HOME GUARD VERSUS THE REGULAR ARMY

Home Guard duties were additional to a full-time job, and they took up a considerable amount of spare-time. But then the war was a round-the-clock affair, in which leisure carried no priority. Regular Sunday church parades were spit-and-polish occasions, so that these and Saturday turn-outs for various Savings Weeks parades took care of many 'free' week-ends.

Then came the real business - week-end field exercises in which the Home Guard were pitted against regular army units to test their mettle. Sunday, 27 July 1941 was a case in point. From 4am regular troops carried out attacks on 19th battalion defences around Bell Green gasworks from prepared positions in Southend Lane. The 'enemy' consisted of units of the Grenadier Guards, Rifle Brigade, Royal West Kents, and West Nova Scotia Regiment. The 19th Battalion were required to prevent these front-line troops capturing the gasworks at all costs in a battle which was just a small part of a much larger exercise.

That very night there occurred a sharp air raid on south east London - the last for many months - in which Sydenham and Penge were bombed. So by Monday morning the local 'Dad's Army' probably thought they had had their fill of action for one week-end.

Later in the war hundreds of local Home Guard were trained in rescue and salvage work in expectation of the V1 flying bomb attacks. But before that they manned London's heavy anti-aircraft guns at night, becoming responsible for the intense barrage of fire which met enemy raiders in 1943 and 1944. On Blackheath Nos 103 and 104 County of London Home Guard Rocket Batteries fired tremendous salvoes of rockets at night intruders. They engaged the enemy in 17 night actions.

If the guns and rockets of London's Home Guard caused damage and disarray in the ranks of the enemy, they terrified the life out of people on the ground. Dad's Army had certainly come a long way since the days of pitchforks.

A Brockley Home Guard Unit at Conisborough Crescent illustrates the great diversity in age of these volunteers. This unit would usually retire to a pub called 'The Brockley Jack' after their Parade.

(Cathy Ransome)

Air Raid Precautions

The letters 'ARP' belonged to that new, arcane vocabulary which grew up in the peculiar circumstances of Britain at war. A kind of newspeak invaded the language - ack-ack and beer-beer, UXBs and Molotovs, NAAFI and ENSA, ATS and WVS, Andersons and Morrisons, Wrens and Waafs, Land Girls and Bevin Boys, AFS, NFS, and EWS, and, just for light relief, ITMA and TTFN....

ARP was the abbreviation for Air Raid Precautions. 'Civil Defence' was a better description, but though this term was officially adopted, it never caught on with the public at the time. Air Raid Wardens were the most visible section of the CD organisation, because they had the closest contact with the general public. For a lot of people the wardens were almost synonymous with the ARP. If anyone said, "He's in the ARP", you could be fairly sure it meant he was a warden.

Wardens' posts were dotted all over Deptford and Lewisham, some in schools, some in purpose-built concrete 'pillboxes'. There were over one hundred, each serving a population of 2,000-3,000 on average. About six wardens normally staffed a post. Most were part-timers, with a full-time job to do as well.

Wardens were an unpopular lot before the bombing started. This was partly because they were responsible for seeing the Black Out rules were obeyed. People uncharitably regarded them as having chosen a nice easy 'number' to avoid doing a real job. One warden told Mass Observation, "I've a good mind to chuck it all up. If there had been an air raid we would all be public heroes. As it is we're called wasters and slackers."

In those days, as a break from daily training and routine, ARP Posts organised darts competitions, parties, amateur shows, table tennis, and billiards. Post A.6 at St Joseph's Academy, Blackheath presented 'Dick Whittington', reported as a "fine performance", helped by an "efficient"

Mum sometimes did my firewatching

A civilian fire-watch was started in our road from six at night to six in the morning, in one hour stints. You hammered on the door of your relief and handed him or her your tin hat before you were allowed to go home yourself. Many's the time in the small hours I would not get up out of bed and my mum did it for me!

Doris Lawrence

Put out fire with Brussels sprouts!

We were in the shelter and there was a man and his son next door to us. They wouldn't come out of their shelter. Their house was on fire with the incendiary bomb, but we went into his garden - of course all the fences were down - where he'd planted all these lovely Brussels sprouts. We shovelled up all his garden, including the Brussels sprouts and all sorts, got buckets and buckets of earth, walked upstairs and put the fire out with the earth and the Brussels sprouts! The man next door wouldn't come out of his shelter because he was scared and he had his son there with him.

Mrs Darling

Lewisham's mobile first aid units attended numerous bomb incidents. For example, No. 2 shown here treated 24 casualties at the V2 rocket blast in Marnock Road, Brockley, 11th February 1945.

2. If out of doors, take off hat, put on your mask. Turn up collar.

Top: The NFS, Army Cadets, Boys Brigade, and others muster in Jerningham Road, New Cross for "Wings for Victory" parade.

Bottom: Sydenham Park ARP wardens Note the WVS member in the back row.

orchestra composed entirely of members of Maylons Road stretcher party. Some started their own house magazines, with evocative titles like 'The Bandage' and 'The Siren'. One in Deptford cheerfully called itself 'Mortuary News'.

None of this seemed to justify the wardens' existence in the eyes of Lewisham ratepayers, especially when they were told in January 1940 that they could "expect the prodigious expenditure involved to be reflected in their rate demands". But the wardens' hour would come. As the man rightly foresaw, they would be public heroes when an air raid occurred.

WARDENS IN THE FRONT-LINE

During air raids the warden would hasten to any 'incident' in his or her area, then phone the ARP Control Centre - located in the basement of the town hall - with details. How many injured? Had anyone been killed? Was anyone trapped? Was anyone missing, perhaps buried in the ruins? If a fire had broken out which could not be handled by those on-the-spot, the warden phoned Fire Control direct for help. All done 'at the double'.

Next return to the scene to assist with whatever tasks most urgently required attention - it might be a fire, it might be helping with first-aid, or assisting the homeless, or trying to release someone trapped... a dozen things to do at once. All the while, Control Centre had to be kept informed on how things were going. If the phones went dead then messengers on motor-cycles were sent with any urgent requests. The pace became really hectic if several incidents occurred together. Since bombs

Shopkeepers shared the firewatching

I did fire-watching at the place where I worked in the Old Kent Road, on the corner of Surrey Square. It had a very deep cellar, so other shop keepers along there used it as a kind of fire-watching head-quarters. Sometimes we had quiet nights and sometimes very hectic nights. I had three or four other shop keepers as companions with me - there were usually four of us. We used to come down once or twice or even three times a week. Other shop keepers took their turn on other nights. All we had to do was just to look after our own premises. At the back of us was the railway goods yard and they had bombs there. There was accidents that happened with bombing around us, and several casualties, but they happened on the nights I wasn't there, fortunately for me. A couple of people were killed right outside the door and then there was a bit of mess and blood on the ground next day. But that all happened on the night it wasn't my turn to be on duty.

Mr Drury snr

fell in 'sticks' of four or six, accompanied by a 'basket' of incendiaries, multiple incidents close together were the rule, rather than the exception.

During the Blitz about 300 wardens lost their lives in London while on duty, together with some 190 in the casualty and rescue services, and those performing fire guard duties. The seriously injured numbered 1,400 and 2,200 respectively. Locally, ARP lives were lost at Clyde Street School (seven died, 17 October 1940); in the street outside Lewisham Town Hall (four killed, 16 April 1941); and Brockley Way ARP Post (four wardens killed, 10 May 1941). There were numerous other tragedies of this kind.

THE BELLS GO DOWN

(Title of war-time film tribute to London firemen)

The need for a volunteer fire force to back up the regular fire brigades was acted upon in 1938 with the formation of the Auxiliary Fire Service. London Fire Brigade (LFB) kept its red fire engines and retained sole responsibility for dealing with 'ordinary' fires. The AFS - using appliances painted in battleship grey, mostly trailer pumps towed by vans, cars and taxis - eventually greatly outnumbered London's professional brigade and played the major role in the Blitz.

At the outbreak of war there were over 20,000 in London's AFS at more than 300 sub-stations. Working alongside the LFB, every man and woman among them would be desperately needed in the great fire raids on the capital. Theirs was among the most dangerous and the most exhausting jobs the war could offer. They could never take it easy simply because things might be quiet in their own district.

Convoys of AFS vehicles would be despatched to fight raging fires wherever help was needed - the City, the docks, the East End, sometimes to the provinces. They might be away for days, returning blackened, saturated, hungry and exhausted. All too often they came back without some of their comrades...

(top) Realistic exercises at Deptford Park Depot for a stretcher party...

(bottom) and for ordinary residents in fire-fighting

Trained to cope with poison gas

I started ARP training in 1938. We were never told there was going to be a war, but they were advertising for people to go and train. I just felt that I could do it. I felt I had to train to help out if there was a war. Mostly it was how to do bandages, how to do little jobs. Most of our training was to do with the gas, how to cope in case we had gas. We had to learn how to get the persons out of the building.

Daisy Cook

"SEND EVERYTHING YOU'VE GOT – THE WHOLE BLOODY WORLD'S ON FIRE."

(Fire Officer's call to Lambeth Fire HQ from Surrey Docks, 7-9-1940)

(top) *Lewisham control centre.*
(bottom) *Deptford control centre plotting the deployment of ARP services.*

Some major fires to which Deptford & Lewisham firemen were sent

Thameshaven Oil Refinery (5-8 Sept. 1940)

Surrey Commercial Docks (7-10 Sept. 1940)

Woolwich Arsenal
(7-8 Sept. 1940 and subsequent dates)

Southampton Docks (10-11 Sept. 1940)

Birmingham (19-21 November 1940)

Manchester (22-24 December 1940)

City of London (29-31 December 1940)

Portsmouth (10-12 January 1941)

Royal Victoria Victualling Yard, Deptford
(19 March 1941)

Elephant & Castle, City of London, etc.
(10-11 May 1941)

On the numerous occasions that local firefighters were ordered to the aid of comrades in other areas others would also have to deal with blazing buildings closer to home. Sometimes they would have to be withdrawn in a hurry from provincial cities because they were needed back again.

During the great docklands raids of 7-8 September 1940 hundreds of crews fought the enormous conflagrations at Surrey Docks and the Woolwich Arsenal. Meanwhile, there were 73 fires in Deptford and New Cross and 92 in various parts of Lewisham which demanded - and got - their urgent attention. Over the next three weeks alone enemy raiders started 700 blazes in Deptford and Lewisham, and by the end of the Blitz the number rose to an estimated 2,100.

THE NATIONAL FIRE SERVICE

In August 1941, after the Blitz ended, the AFS and all the nation's regular fire brigades were merged to form one national organisation, the National Fire Service (NFS). This force was organised and trained to a high standard of efficiency and professionalism. It was better equipped than the old AFS had been with its motley collection of pumps and towing machines. Their smart, grey Bedford lorries became a familiar sight in the streets after 1941. And now, of course, the fire engines and turntables of the LFB were crewed by men wearing the NFS uniform, though under the uniforms, no doubt, they were the same men as before.

No one survived the fire

I used to go out with the doctors and help them. You would have to help them as they were tending to the patients as they came out from the rubble. We went to one house and I think it was in Shell Road where we had to stand guard because the house was all on fire. The firemen were spraying hoses and people were trapped in the basements. The bomb had come down and fell not far from where we was standing, but I don't think they ever got them poor people out.

Daisy Cook

We bandaged them up

On the Sunday the warning went and of course we had been told that if there was a warning we had to report at once, so straight away then I lost my job at the brewery - I had been there nine years. I had to go straight away to report to the first aid post. I didn't even have to give notice. Our post was at Harton Street - that is in the Broadway - and we went from there to Goldsmiths' College. I was in Goldsmiths' College when they dropped the baskets of fire bombs all over the college. We was ordered to get out into the field in case it became dangerous. We were called out to New Cross Station when that had been bombed. I used to go then on the ambulance to help these emergency doctors. I just helped to bandage anyone up, or run messages, because I wasn't qualified. I did first aid. I had to help where ever I could help, but you saw some nasty bombings during that time.

Changing shift saved her life

Where I was stationed in Deptford, we had quite a few different people in with us of different kinds like Methodists and Salvation Army. One night, I'd changed shifts with this young Salvation Army girl. She was doing my shift because she was going to a wedding the next day. And that same night the whole post was bombed to the ground. It was a land mine. When I reported to work the next morning, the road had all been roped off. The police came and told me that I had to report at the Town Hall. Well they were a bit surprised when I got to the Town Hall because they thought I was still there - I was told they was still looking for me because they knew that was my shift. But that poor girl was killed and most of the people I was working with at the time.

Daisy Cook

Spent whole night carrying bodies from Woolworth's

I was returning home from Deptford Central Library and was walking in Malpas Road when the explosion occurred. I knew exactly what it was, having been involved in the Shardeloes Road incident some three weeks earlier.

I was a messenger attached to Post 17 in Brockley. I reported for duty at around 1800. The duty warden told me that our Deputy Post Warden, Bob Tatum, was at the incident with three or four of our wardens.

When bodies were recovered from the debris, as soon as it was established that they were dead, they were put into hessian shrouds and carted across the road to Pearce Signs which was being used as a temporary mortuary. I carted corpses with a warden from Giffin Street almost non-stop from about 1900 to 0300 on the Sunday.

Many of the corpses recovered had very severe crushing injuries and were oozing blood which soon seeped through the hessian shrouds. There was blood everywhere, much more than I had ever seen before or since. Some corpses had quite benign expressions and some features as if contorted with horror.

Looking back, it seems to me impossible to convey to someone who did not experience it just what it was like. In some ways it all seemed unreal. There was an ever-present sense of danger. Most of the time the weather was cold, but it seemed that however cold it was we were always perspiring and always covered in brick dust. Many of us at times worked twenty hours a day and were usually pretty weary.

Les Harling

(Reprinted with permission from Rations and Rubble, Deptford Forum Publishing, 1994)

NFS Fire Stations

The main fire stations were the peace-time LFB stations at:

- Queen's Road, New Cross,
- Perry Vale, Forest Hill,
- Lewisham High Street, Ladywell,
- Eltham Road, Lee,
- Evelyn Street, Deptford.

Sub-stations were in schools at:

Turnham Road	Aske's Girls'	Brownhill Road
Monson Road	Albyn Road	Sandhurst Road
Morden Terrace	Adamsrill Road	Baring Road
Sydenham County	Forest Hill Central	Beacon Road
Stillness Road	Lewisham Bridge	Pendragon Road
Gordonbrock Road	Torridon Road	Leahurst Road

and Kangley Bridge Road (a factory)

The NFS Training School was at Flower House, Southend.

The Blitz had taken a heavy toll on London's AFS. Not simply from deaths and injuries through enemy action, which were worse than for some front-line troops, but also from illness, exhaustion, and other after-effects of relentless exposure to extremes of cold and heat, to smoke and burning embers, loss of sleep, hunger, and prolonged periods spent soaked to the skin.

They emerged from this crucible of hardship intensely proud of their achievements and with a powerful sense of comradeship. Those who transferred to it probably never felt quite the same way about the NFS. There was a strong ex-naval presence in London's fire services, and they say sailors who lose their first ship never feel the same way about her replacement.

However that may be, the NFS went on to earn the highest regard and deep gratitude of the people of Deptford and Lewisham. This was especially the case during the V1 flying bomb and V2 rocket campaigns. Firemen played the leading role in Civil Defence in 1944 and 1945. They were usually the first on the scene, for they could spot the explosions from their observation posts. Almost before the dust had settled, a self-contained column of NFS crews would arrive on the spot. They immediately set about rescuing trapped victims, salvaging property, giving first-aid, patching up damaged houses.... Their mere presence brought reassurance and restored morale.

This is not to overlook the splendid and hazardous work done by the rescue and casualty services throughout those trying months. The release

New Cross Road was like a battlefield

I was in the Civil Defence based at Nynehead Street School. We used to have to do so many hours a week down there, part time. We were only volunteers. I was walking down Woodpecker Road coming home from being at work and there was a mighty crash-bang-wallop, things flying everywhere, lucky I didn't get caught on anything. I thought, "Now, that's near." Carried on home, got changed into uniform and went out. I met someone who said, "It's New Cross Road, it's Woolworth's that's gone." I'd got my bike so it only took me a few minutes but when you got up there you wanted to turn around and come back because it was just like a battlefield, people laying in the road and rubble everywhere. But you do a doubletwist and come to your senses and you know that you've got to do it.

You'd go to people who were injured first. We commandeered a coach of sailors and used it as an ambulance until the real ambulances arrived. All the sailors mucked in, climbing on the rubble and trying to get people out. Those that were screaming you tried to get to them and get them out before their injuries got worse.

We helped to get people out, not just the bodies but those that were injured. As it got dark they set up a

Members of Lewisham's Heavy Rescue Squad, whose main depot was at Wearside Road, Ladywell. They were needed at 73 incidents in the first four days of the Blitz alone, when they succeeded in rescuing 55 persons alive from under collapsed buildings Mr. Bernard Bennie who won the George Medal at Catford is seen in the back row, third from the right.

of people buried under tons of debris called for the skills and courage of specialist teams of rescue workers. Similarly, only mobile medical units, with trained doctors and nurses, could provide proper treatment for the injured.

Nor is it to overlook the fact that the NFS still had fires to fight. Any fires at a bomb blast would be their first priority, but they were certainly assisted by the well-organised system of fireguards. It was the duty of employees to spend one night a week guarding their place of work against incendiary bombs. Some streets organised volunteer fireguards of their own. So it was that in the 'Baby Blitz' of 1944, when some 600 fires were started in Deptford and Lewisham, fewer than 100 called for the involvement of the NFS. These latter were, of course, the big ones, such as a 50-pump timber and creosote inferno at St Andrew's Wharf, Deptford.

THE WOMEN'S VOLUNTARY SERVICE

("A triumph of patriotism and the voluntary principle")

Their full title was 'Women's Voluntary Services for Civil Defence'. They were entirely dedicated to helping to win the war. That is what the WVS was set-up for, and for no other reason. It would fill a book to describe all the tasks with which the members became involved. 'Involved' is not quite strong enough a word to describe their contribution. Whatever the task, they threw themselves into it with energy and determination.

By 1942 Deptford and Lewisham could boast a WVS army numbering several thousands. They worked as nursing auxiliaries, hospital work parties, ARP wardens, ambulance and fire appliance drivers.... They staffed control centres and first-aid posts, served as shelter marshals, ran rest and feeding centres for the bombed-out, served in canteens, assisted with evacuation, organised salvage drives, and ran street savings groups... But this is not the full list. In fact, one of their primary tasks was to act as a recruiting agency for the other ARP services.

Before the Blitz began, 1,000 Lewisham WVS called on all households

portacabin and once they started getting a few names through of injured people, the three of us working in there made lists out. Then of course people were coming up saying, "My wife's gone out shopping and she's not returned home," people wanting to know if Mrs Brown's on the list. That carried on all night long. Our neighbour Curly, his mother got killed there and Curly was up there with his Dad. He was only a little boy then with the peaked cap round the side, looking up. And his father was saying, "Find my wife, find my wife, I'll give you anything."

Ethel Long

(Reprinted with permission from Rations and Rubble, Deptford Forum Publishing, 1994)

in the borough in a great salvage drive for pots, pans and kettles needed as metal scrap. In July 1940 the Queen visited Heathfield House, Eliot Place, Blackheath to inspect the work of the hospital supplies section. By then over 10,000 garments for the sick and wounded had been distributed from the centre.

From their store in St Mary's School, Ladywell, the WVS clothed over 3,000 families who had lost everything in the Blitz. They ran eight rest and feeding centres in the borough, mostly located in church halls, though they themselves were bombed out of their base in Christ Church and had to move to 7, Catford Road.

The vast majority of these women had full-time responsibilities elsewhere. They were unpaid for their services, and even had to pay for their own uniforms, using up their own precious clothing coupons into the bargain. Whenever the authorities found a new job needing to be done, they turned to the WVS to do it. Their tasks multiplied month by month. Caring for the troops after Dunkirk? Leave it to the WVS. Street firefighting parties? The WVS will organise them. Clothing stores for the bombed out? Volunteer car pools, for use in an emergency? Enquiry points at major bomb incidents? The Home Front could hardly have coped without the WVS in their sensible, country-tweed suits.

Sporting personalities form stretcher party in Deptford. From left to right: - Ron Johnson, Australian member of New Cross Speedway, - Tommy Martin, Deptford Heavyweight Boxer, - Jack Croly, Millwall Cruiserweight Boxer, - Stafford Barton, Middleweight Champion of Jamaica.

AGS Messenger too exhausted to return home

In September 1940, my fifteen year old brother was a messenger with the Auxiliary Fire Service. When he didn't arrive home in the early hours of the morning, following the all-clear, we were all worried. We went out locally, walking the streets, but couldn't find him, so my father went down to the AFS station, and was told that he had in fact left after the all-clear. My father decided to have a look round the building and found him fast asleep on a heap of coke! They told my father he had worked very hard and was obviously so exhausted he just couldn't manage to walk home.

Margaret Kippin

A . R . P .
Shatter Resisting Mixture
The perfect window protection against blast and shrapnel splinters

ESSENTIAL TO FIRE WATCHERS

AIR RAID FIRST AID

Terror from the sky

What a single mine could do - Milton Court Road, Deptford, 22nd September 1940. Much of the remaining housing was destroyed in subsequent attacks.

When Dad Got Killed…

I went to dinner in a coffee shop you know and I was sitting down at a table and someone turned round and said to me, "That was a bad turn out at Lewisham this morning, wasn't it?" So I said, "What's that then, mate?" He said, "It's a doodlebug landed on Marks and Spencers." Well, that was where my dad and mum worked, right there, on their fruit stall. Of course I come home to see what had happened. When I got back here Dad had been killed by this doodlebug. The doodlebug had glided in and it was a bit of a misty morning in July and it caught the edge of the steeple and it turned it round down into the

High Street. It was a bad turn out, it was bad. They only found half of Dad, and his motor was about 40 or 50 yards away, and it was blown to pieces, bits and pieces.

They was a devoted couple. She was never the same, never the same after that. Funny thing, if she hadn't had a hole in that pocket she would have very likely gone and all. She stopped indoors, she says "I won't be long Harry, I won't be long, " she says, "I'll just mend this hole in this pocket and then I'll be out." In the meantime the bloody doodlebug come in and that was that, no more. There was about 50 odd people killed that day.

When Dad got killed I just walked out of my job with the council and told them down Deptford High Street, that I wouldn't go back for nobody. I come back and looked after Mum and the stall.

Jim Jeal
(Lewisham Street Trader)

Marks and Spencer's Was Ablaze

They never heard that doodlebug coming in because it cut out a long way out and they glide in don't they? It came down right in front of Marks and Spencers, and quite a few of the old ones got killed that day including our grandad. He never heard it coming. One of the young ones, he was packing out down there, and he managed to get down the shelter when it went off. He come out and all the girls that was up the top of Marks and Spencers changing to go to work they was diving out of the windows. It was blazing.

The Sky Was Black With Bombers

That tragic day on the Saturday morning, there was me and another party packing out our stalls on the market, and they come over here after they'd done Biggin Hill. The sky was full of them coming in. They was like flies coming over - just like flies they was - the sky was black with them. One bomb drops on that building over there next to the church. It belonged to the Electric Light Company, and one dropped where British Home Stores is now. There was a big warehouse there where you would go down the stairs in the front. We ran

Top Left: Lewisham Hospital suffered a direct hit by a V1 flying bomb.
Top Right: Hither Green Station. The blast of a V1 in Nightingale Grove killed five passengers on the platform.

Sandhurst Road School, Catford, one of the war's most notorious incidents. A direct hit in daylight on 20th January 1943 cost the lives of 38 children and six teachers 60 more children were seriously injured.

Top: Blackheath Village shattered by a V2 rocket in Wemyss Road, 8th March 1945. Every shop and building suffered some damage. Five lives were lost and 134 people were injured.

Far Right: One of the country's worst V1 blasts devastated Lewisham Shopping Centre, 28th July 1944. With 51 people killed and 311 injured, the scene was described as worse than a battlefield. The bomb missed underground shelters by a few yards, thereby avoiding an even greater death toll.

Bottom: A mine that went off while being defused in Oldstead Road, Downham, 17th November 1940. Everyone had been evacuated previously.

down there and that bomb came down and hit the Electric Light Company. No traffic could come through, there was debris all over the road, but they never touched the church, that's still there today, the church.

**'Bonk' Walkling
(Lewisham Street Trader)**

Went Hop-picking When The Bombing Was Bad

I had one son born in '41, another one born in '43. We lived down Legge Street. When the rockets started, my husband and I took the two boys down the shelter in the garden and we sat up all night because we didn't know what they were. Well, then that day, in the lunchtime, one came down quite near us and knocked all the ceilings down and blew the door off.

Before the war like we used to go down to the hopfields in Kent and my Grandad used to cook fish and chips down there. There was a big pub called the Bluebell at Beltring Halt near Paddock Wood and it had loads of ground. We were allowed to sell fish and chips to the hop-pickers there. I was only young and I used to have a cockle and whelk stall. I never used to pick hops.

When the bombing got very bad in the war, Grandad took us hopping. We went down the hop fields and we picked hops, you know. He said, "Do you girls want to come to Maidstone?", so we said, "Yes, alright, we'll come with you." So we went to Maidstone. We went down the toilet and the siren went and the lady said,

"Oh you haven't got to worry, we don't get nothing here," and that was the day that they were fighting all overhead and dropping bombs everywhere. Well we were very lucky because we got shoved down under these arches and we were safe although a bomb fell very near. So then when it was a bit clear we went and found Grandad and he took us home, but on the way home driving he had to keep stopping and sort of hiding because there was nothing but machine-gunning going on. So it was quite exciting really but not very nice is it?

Mrs Waving

Walked The Streets All Night

We was at Blackhorse Road and we got bombed out. The first time we got bombed out one of the aunts put us up, there was six of us. Because one of my sisters had whooping cough she wouldn't put us up no more so she kicked us out. So we walked the streets all night. I was about four. I remember going in a big hall with stacks of kids and everyone is crying and everything. This was at the beginning of the war, 1940. Then we was evacuated, but we couldn't get on down there and they treated us terrible so the old man brought us home. He said, "I've got a house for you at Bellingham." He brought us straight home, put us in there and he went down the pub. He put us in this house and he disappeared. It was like a palace: stairs and a bath. We said, "It's got a bath and a toilet!" A garden. We was over the moon. You couldn't afford to put anything in them. There was no lino, nothing.

Richard White

Bombed Out And Left To Cope

It just happened, like a big clap of thunder, as if a thunderbolt had come down. I had to inform the rest of the family that were at work. And just get along. By which time the neighbours had said, "Now come along. It's all right." They fortunately had spare bedrooms in their house. You just had to manage from then on. I did go to the authorities at the old Deptford Town Hall, just in Lewisham Road, and asked what would be available and they were very non-committal. They inquired where we were living and I told her and they were quite happy about that - because you'd got somewhere and so why worry any more about you. "Had I got any money? Could I get at any money?" "Yes." "Oh well then, we shan't bother." And they didn't. Didn't worry about us at all, so we just had to pull ourselves together and pick up the pieces.

Miss Applegate

Home Sweet Home. It took a life-time for working people to build up a home, only to have it reduced to rubble and a bundle of clothes - Arica Road, Brockley, 17th January 1943. 20 people died here and in Howson Road.

The open space is where Woolworth's store stood in New Cross Road, the site of Britain's most calamitous V2 Rocket incident at least 160 people perished here, including many women and children doing some early Christmas shopping, 25th November 1944.

They Hid Under The Privets When Machine-Gunned

In the morning there was an aeroplane that came over, a very red aeroplane, and the man was looking out. We didn't realise it was a German one, it was a little red aeroplane. He came ever so low. I was banging my mats and talking to my neighbour and suddenly the thing came over so low that, with the rush of air, my mats went on the floor. I was ever so annoyed. That was the day Sandhurst Road School was bombed. He was a wicked man who ever he was. I hope his conscience pricks him for as long as he lives, because he come around and he was machine gunning the children that was playing. We had to get right under the edges of the privets, push the kids under the privets to hide. I was dead scared. I had three of the children with me then, and they were going to see "Over the Rainbow", they was going to meet to go on the tram to Lewisham Hippodrome.

My husband was working at Catford police station and several of the policemen had their children attending that school. It was like a nightmare the whole time, but my husband helped to get the dead children out. There was quite a lot.

Mrs Darling

There Was This Terrific Crash....

We lived in the bottom of Malpas Road then. I just got home from work and sat down in the arm chair. I lived on the top floor then. All of a sudden there was this terrific crash and the lights all went out, the ceiling all came down, the party wall of the two rooms came in, the window panes were blown all across the other side of the room. Two front doors, one down in the basement and one at the top, they were blown right up to the bottom of the stairs, torn off the hinges right at the bottom of the stairs. That was the most damage that we received except for broken windows before that. And no slates on the roof.

Mr Drury snr

Parents Were Going Mad At Sandhurst Road

I took the oxygen bottles and the cutting equipment out to Sandhurst Road School with another chap and people was going mad. Mothers and fathers trying to find their children under the debris. I never want to see that again. Poor little kids. We want to live happy. We don't want to be fighting one another. Why couldn't He have stopped all that. He's supposed to have all this power. There never has been a God, mate, and there never will be one. There never will be one.

Another bad turn out was on Clarendon Rise, a direct hit there. There was some shelters down there you know and there'd been some bombing and they had to divert the buses and all the traffic round and come down Clarendon Rise - they was in a terrible state they was. I was working on the council then. Oh me, that was terrible. People was absolutely blown to pieces. Well they didn't really clear the place out, they just filled it in. Chaps I know on the council they all went down in vans and lorries and all that to clear it out a bit so's they could see what had happened and they couldn't do it. They was all blown to pieces. It was a terrible day it was.

Jim Jeal

A sheltered life

The war brought radical alterations to the landscape in Deptford and Lewisham. To the skyscape, too, if one thinks of the barrage balloons, which hung up there like "lots of little elephants", as one old lady put it. The balloons are a story in themselves. But on the ground it was the construction of air raid shelters which produced some of the more intrusive changes.

Unsightly mounds of earth in nearly everyone's back garden revealed the presence of domestic Anderson shelters. These were made of corrugated, galvanised steel sheets, bolted together and placed over a trench in the ground, three feet (one metre) deep. The curved top was then covered by earth to a depth of about eighteen inches (half a metre). A very cheap and effective form of protection, the Anderson turned out to be. Except that it was prone to flooding on clay soil in wet weather.

Andersons were provided free to those on incomes of less than £5 per week, which was practically everybody. They cost £7 to those on higher incomes, but such purchases were ruled out until the demand for free shelters had been satisfied. By May 1940, 9,100 Deptford gardens contained them, and only seven had been bought. Lewisham's figure was about 23,000. In total they could accommodate 195,000 people at a pinch, according to the official yardstick of six persons to a shelter. That was quite a squeeze, although it was not unknown for eight or nine persons to crowd into one for the night.

For flat-dwellers and others without a private garden, communal surface shelters were generally provided. These were of a 'pillbox' design - oblong blocks of brick and concrete or lime mortar. The lime mortar versions proved useless against blast and had to be replaced. Deptford constructed 95 surface brick shelters for the use

No Chance To Shelter

The procedure in those days was that the warning used to go and the assistants from the stores, from Marks and Sparks and all the big stores, were turned out and went into the shelters. There was a series of shelters on what was known as the Green in those days - underground shelters and also shelters in Avenue Road. Whenever the warning went, the buses, public transport, used to stop, turn all the public off to take shelter. Well, in the end it became a bit of a joke really because nothing ever happened but then, on that Saturday concerned, it did happen.

When we heard the warning, we used to cover the market stalls up, empty the tills, get a sheet over the stalls and go down the shelters. On that particular day I remember clearing up with my mother and father, putting the sheets over the stalls and we went down the shelter. Prior to going there I looked up, being a young adventurous young man in those days and the Jerries were coming, and they were just like ants in the sky, wave after wave after wave.

The Electric Light Company in Lewisham was the first casualty. They

Air raid siren at the top of Westwood Hill, Sydenham. The concerted blare of about 25 such sirens in Deptford and Lewisham sent residents to take cover on over 1,200 occasions.

of flat-dwellers, but the same type was also erected in some residential streets for the use of casual passers-by 'caught out' in an air raid.

Shelters for general public use commonly took the form of deep trenches covered by strong timbers and earth. A wall of sandbags protected the entrance and a short flight of steps descended into the interior, which, with a bit of luck, would contain electric lights in working order and wooden benches lining the walls. Such shelters were constructed in, or adjacent to, busy thoroughfares, often on the edge of public parks. By May 1940 Deptford possessed public shelters for over 12,000 people, including trenches for 5,000 in Deptford Park. In Lewisham, trenches existed in the gardens and lawns of the High Street near Lewisham Hospital and in Rushey Green. Others were excavated in the grounds of Robertson's Golden Shred works in Bromley Road. Those uncovered recently near the Clock Tower were intended to accommodate several hundred short-stay shelterers. Wall markings show where wooden benches were fixed and other signs indicate the installation of bunks at a later date.

UNDERNEATH THE ARCHES

'They're building flats where the arches used to be', the London comedians, Flanagan and Allen, sang as a sequel to their famous number, 'Underneath The Arches'. Had they composed the sequel a few years later, it would have surely been, 'They're building air raid shelters where the arches used to be'.

Neither Deptford nor Lewisham were as dependent upon railway arches for public shelter accommodation as nearby Bermondsey but they did play their part. Quite simply the sides of the arches were bricked-up, apart from a space to enter, and the existing structure provided the rest of the protection. They were no good against a direct hit - then neither was any other kind of shelter, except the basements of large buildings and those deep underground.

A Reinforced Concrete Air Raid Shelter: It has been built in the garden of Mrs H. C. Davies in Hilly Fields Crescent, Brockley. Mrs Davies is seen in this posed picture as she takes in emergency stores. The shelter has been built to meet Home Office requirements, the walls being a foot thick

spent a long time building it, but it didn't take long to knock it down, unfortunately. And it all went wrong from there. The raids continued and there were a lot of bombings in the area where the markets were concerned.

Unfortunately the poor souls that were killed on the market the day the VI landed there had no warning. This VI came over had cut out way back, glided right over Kent, glided in and then dropped on the market. The warning hadn't gone, and that's why the casualty list was so high - had they been down the shelter it would have been a lot better you know, a lot would have survived.

Mr Davis
(Lewisham Street Trader)

Public shelters initially lacked bunks and sanitation. They were without heating, of course, and there was no water supply - except when the rain found a way in.

Garden Anderson shelters were equally primitive and were referred to as 'dug-outs', after the trenches in the First World War. They at least would have bunks installed, and the occupants could always nip indoors during a lull in the bombing to make a pot of tea or to use the toilet. Morrison indoor shelters eventually provided the answer to most of the drawbacks mentioned, but these did not become available until after the Blitz. The Morrison consisted of a sturdy metal cage with meshed sides which could be adapted to double-up as a table. It was supposed to withstand the weight of the house collapsing on it.

Numerous local residents, particularly those driven out of their homes, took up semi-permanent abode in the deep passages and caverns of Chislehurst Caves. Every evening trains on the line through New Cross, Hither Green and Grove Park were filled with families on their way to Chislehurst to claim their pitches. Others caught the connecting 227 bus service from Bromley Market Square. Lewisham Borough News reported that large numbers used the caves as a dormitory, with one woman telling Catford Citizens Advice Bureau that "they were very comfortable there in an alcove reserved for them".

In July 1941, when London had been raid-free for two months, some 2,000 still lived in the caves at night. The Borough News remarked, "The nightly trek via Hither Green station is now less conspicuous, but some mothers and children still go". The caves had two great advantages over all other shelters: they were safe against direct hits and they allowed a decent sleep, uninterrupted by the un-nerving sounds of the nightly raids.

"SHELTER SIDELIGHTS"

Regular users of the same public shelter got to know one another in time and a rudimentary social life often took shape. During the winter of 1940-1941 the Kentish Mercury featured a series on the subject which it called 'Shelter Sidelights'. Amateur concerts, parties, gramophone music, whist drives, French lessons, sing-songs, and even 'house' magazines were organised among the larger congregations. Such activities helped pass the time pleasantly, while taking minds off the fears and anxieties which everyone privately nursed. In the close working class communities of places like Deptford and the LCC estates they effectively kept up local traditions of communal enjoyment normally centred on pubs and working men's clubs.

But none of it could hide the fact that death and destruction lurked overhead. For much of the time during an all-night raid the threat was in the background. Things might be quiet for an hour or more at a time. It varied. No two raids were exactly alike, so you could not tell what might happen. Outside in the Black Out a few searchlights wavering about in the distant sky... the red glow of a fire somewhere, started by a previous wave of bombers... maybe the passing of ambulances and fire appliances attending an incident nearby.

Silence was not reassuring. It was ominous. At any moment it could be broken by the rumble of distant gunfire, growing louder and nearer by the moment... until the dull throbbing of bombers at great height could be heard approaching. Now came the test. Would they drop their bombs or would they keep them for somewhere else? It took more than a sing-song to take the mind off what might happen next....

Railway Arches Adapted As Shelters

Location	No. Accommodated
Deptford Market	550
Loampit Hill Bridge	150
Ravensbourne Park	60
Catford Hill Bridge	105
Morley Road Bridge	95
Plough Bridge	40

Taunton Road, Lee. - VE Day Celebration, with typical street surface shelter in the background .

Shared Anderson With Mother-in-Law

I lived next door to my mother-in-law in Friendly Street, Deptford. They knocked a part of the fence down so we shared the shelter with her. It was a case of nipping through the garden fence to the Anderson shelter. You went down there and then when it was all quiet you went back to bed.

This is the strange thing - there was a family in an Anderson shelter near us and a heavy bomb fell right near where they were. The strange thing was - they were all killed because they were sitting up. It was the blast that broke their necks.

Gladys Barratt

Slept Under The Dining Table

There wasn't a shelter round here to which you could go. There was one dug into the ground in the garden of the house but it wasn't suitable to use. It was just like a hole in the ground with corrugated over the top. You just slept where you thought you would be safest in the house. Before we were burnt down we had a large mahogany dining table in one of the rooms. I used to sleep under there, keeping awake as much as we could during the night. And the others just had mattresses, blankets, whatever, on the floor.

Miss Applegate

Kept Awake By The Guns

Dad had a brick shelter built under the shop at 252 Brockley Road - I presume it's still there now. It had six bunks, three bunks each side, an opening in the centre. We used to go in there. Sometimes, if the raids were really bad, they had guns on Hilly Fields. There was a gunsite where the putting green is now, near the school. When it was really bad they would be coming over in droves. They used to send mobile guns out in the streets and if they went off, you couldn't get any sleep because they'd be mobile guns on lorries, firing - "Boom! boom!" - and you was in the shelter.

So we didn't get any sleep. It wasn't so bad for us, but more for Mum and Dad because they still had to keep going to run the shop.

Pat McDonald

Chislehurst Caves

When we got there, my father parked his lorry up on a hillside sloping. Then we went across into the caves. It smelt all musty and damp, from the chalk. All the front of the caves and the centre were taken by people that had beds up. They used to use a frying pan with a candle under it to fry a sausage, somebody did, because there were no cooking facilities there. People used to take flasks and sandwiches. They made beds up. There were lights, but not many. Just the main one down there. If you were under the side or in a corner, it would be dark. We had to go right to the back of the cave because all the fronts were taken by regulars. My father came with us but because of his breathing problems he wouldn't go again.

Pat McDonald

Go Back To Your Own Shelters!

My brother-in-law who hadn't yet been called up for the army because of his age, he started taking us to different shelters - in Eden Park, Beckenham - but some of the residents complained and when they found out where we were from said we had a cheek coming and taking their shelters away from them.

One night my sister got up and had a row with them. When we first arrived it was daylight and they were all saying, "Where are you from?" and we were saying, "From Brockley." They were going, "Oh." When it got to night-time we could hear them saying, "Damn cheek coming down here, taking our places away. Taking our shelters from us."

Pat McDonald

The Mattress Was Afloat

We dug our own shelter, I borrowed my husband's trousers, because in those days it was dreadful to see a woman walking out in trousers. I put my husband's trousers on and started digging, and then all the women helped each other dig. Then the people came, from Lewisham or some authority, they came and put the shelters up and we covered them over with earth and all that sort of thing, but of course they weren't waterproof.

We put mattresses on the floor. One night when we went to put the kids to bed there, the mattress was floating - it was the water. It was bad. Well then, after that, they lined it with concrete half way up. If there was a raid on, I would nip around to the shops because I lived at the back of the shops and they was always empty during a raid so you could get your little bits of what you wanted.

Mrs Darling

They Stayed In Bed

The nearest shelter to where I lived was about 300 yards away. If you were in the factory most people just carried on working. If the raids were during the night my mum would say, "Come on, get up. There's a raid. We're going down the shelter." I'd say, "Mum, I've got to get up and work in the morning." My brother said the same. The other two were evacuated. We'd say "I've got to get up and work in the morning. I'm not going to get up and run down the shelter in my night clothes for about 300 yards and then come back again and go to be,. disturb the night". So we didn't bother. My eldest brother slept in the attic and he didn't bother either.

Lill Murrell

Safer Than Houses

It was a very very long garden and there was a shed at the bottom and this shelter was built like a shop would be built, all iron, and a good thing it was, because we had a hundred pound bomb at the bottom of the garden. We had three bunks in there. I was sleeping on the top bunk. The guns used to go whoosh!! whoosh!! in my ear, through the little air duct. We heard this awful blast and we thought the house had gone and we couldn't wait for the all clear to go to open the door. And in came glass and rubble. The house was still there but there wasn't a window anywhere, and lots of brick had come out and the wall that was round it was all blown up. When we looked down the garden there was no shed and of course my bike was in there and the lawn mower. Do you know where they found it? Right over the tops of the houses, in the church gardens - my bicycle all tangled up, and the lawn mower, the roller. They were blown over into the church garden. You can imagine the blast of it. And we were still intact in our shelter.

Susan Swann

45

Fighting The 'Squander Bug'

People's incomes were heavily taxed to help pay for the enormous costs of the war. The standard rate of tax shot up from 25 per cent to 37 $\frac{1}{2}$ per cent soon after hostilities commenced. In 1940 it was raised again to 42 $\frac{1}{2}$ per cent, and then to 50 per cent in 1941. The war made a big hole in everyone's pocket.

To make sure the taxman received his slice of earnings without delay or evasion, the Pay As You Earn (PAYE) system was fully implemented in 1944. Under this method the earners' wages are taken away at source and they never get the chance to spend the money on themselves, which has always made it popular with the authorities.

Despite the high level of taxes, including purchase tax introduced in 1940 (33 $\frac{1}{3}$ per cent on luxuries and 16 $\frac{2}{3}$ per cent on a range of essentials), only about a half of the war's costs were met in this way. Most of the difference had to come from government borrowings, and here is where the National Savings movement entered the picture.

National Savings had its own little creature for propaganda purposes. It was called the SQUANDER BUG - a nasty, persistent little germ. The symptoms of infection by it were that you spent any spare cash you might have on unnecessary things, instead of putting it in National Savings. It was portrayed as helping Hitler to win the war, for its sole aim in life was to sabotage our own war efforts by urging us to SPEND.

It was temptation itself to self-indulgence. "Go on, Mum", the Squander Bug whispered in the shopper's ear, "treat yourself to a new coat."

Deptford Town Hall During 'Warships Week' "We're here because the Navy's There' says the placard. £500,000 appears to be the target

"Selfish expenditure and its bad effects on the economy has shown little sign of being generally heeded."

(Complaint of the National Savings Committee, Christmas 1942)

NO STREET SHOULD BE WITHOUT ONE - A SAVINGS GROUP

Form A Savings Group In Your Factory, Office, Workshop, Store or Club.

- National Savings poster in 1940.

Every week on pay-day (Friday) an appointed trustworthy person toured the work-place collecting sixpences and half-crowns in exchange for savings stamps. The intention was that when an employee had stuck sufficient stamps into the little folder supplied, he or she would take them along to the post office and swap them for a savings certificate.

The beauty of the scheme was that workers could be approached as soon as they had received their pay packets and were feeling well-off for the moment. Monday was too late in the work-place. That was the 'feel bad' day, financially and in other respects. But the savings cause was not lost even then. By setting up street savings groups, much of the wages could be pursued after it had become housekeeping money in the wife's purse.

At the urging of the Chancellor of the Exchequer, local mayors and Members of Parliament campaigned in 1940 for the formation of street savings groups. The procedure was similar to that in factories and offices: somebody trustworthy in the street, very often a member of the Women's Voluntary Service, did the door-to-door selling, usually at the week-end, and accounted for the funds to the National Savings Committee. By May 1940 over £400,000 had been saved in Lewisham by this means, and in 1942 there were groups in

Baring Road, Grove Park lends a hand with Lewisham's War Weapons Week', May 1941

LEWISHAM'S

WINGS FOR VICTORY WEEK

MARCH 6th-13th

Target - £750,000

to purchase

FOUR-ENGINED
18 STIRLING BOMBERS
6 SPITFIRE FIGHTERS

PROGRAMME—

Lewisham Civil Defence Artists' Exhibition at Horniman Museum, Forest Hill, opened by W. Russell Flint, Esq., R.A., President Royal Watercolour Society.

Prize Exhibition of Model Aircraft, Soft Toys, Knitting and Needlework, together with other valuable Models at The Fifty Shilling Tailors, 200, High Street, Lewisham.

Grand Procession of Detachments of Air Force, other Military Forces, Home Guard, Civil Defence, Cadet Corps, Boy Scouts, Girl Guides, Youth Clubs, etc., on Saturday, March 6th.

Church Parade at Lewisham Hippodrome on Sunday, March 7th, at which The Lord Bishop of Woolwich and Maj.-Gen. The Rt. Hon. Lord Mottistone, C.B., C.M.G., D.S.O., will speak.

Auction of Works of Art, given by exhibitors at Horniman Museum, Saturday, March 13th, by Henry Brooke, Esq., M.P.

Presentation of Prizes and Certificates of Merit at the Town Hall, by The Mayoress, Saturday, March 13th.

Also Whist Drives, Dances, Keep Fit and Dancing Display, etc., throughout the Week.

Souvenir Brochures on Sale, Price 2d., giving full particulars of all events throughout the week. Proceeds given to defray expenses.

ALL INFORMATION FROM
WINGS OFFICE, 1, CATFORD

48

---

475 out of 1010 streets in the borough. Remnants of the system lived on in rural areas until the 1980s, when it was formally wound up as uneconomic.

PUTTING SOME EXCITEMENT INTO SAVINGS

Let's face it: saving is boring, as well as unpopular. The National Savings movement understood that, so it came up with the idea of Savings Weeks in order to put some kick into the drab business, while at the same time giving an annual boost to local collections.

Every town and borough throughout the country was regularly required to organise a Savings week, with the theme chosen and promoted by the central organisers of the National Savings movement. Local boroughs decided on their own targets for new savings, and it seemed to be understood that the target should be one which could be comfortably exceeded.

A certain amount of civic pride and competition was injected into the proceedings, so that no borough should feel out-done by the efforts of neighbours of similar size and wealth. In May 1941 Lewisham set itself a target of £250,000 for War Weapons Week, actually raising £688,000. This meant a target of £700,000 the following year for Warships Week, "to buy a destroyer".

All manner of activities were promoted during the week in support of new savings - concerts, displays, exhibitions, dances, whist drives, art and music competitions.... in a welter of publicity for the cause. Most boroughs erected a 'thermometer' in a prominent spot which was updated daily showing progress towards the target. Both Lewisham and Deptford placed theirs outside the town halls. The climax of the week came with a celebratory 'victory' procession through the town centre, to the applause of waiting crowds. Every kind of uniformed organisation would be represented, including the armed services and Civil Defence, with several military bands adding colour and drama to the occasion.

War Weapons Weeks	-	Sept. 1940 - October 194
Warships Weeks		Oct. 1941 - March 1942
Wings For Victory Weeks		Spring and Summer 1943
Salute The Soldier Weeks-		March 1944-July 1944

Is Your Journey Really Necessary?

Every bit of capacity of Britain's railway system was required for troop movements and the transportation of war supplies. Passenger services faced a lower priority. These were sharply curtailed at the outbreak of war, and those still left in the timetable were subject to delay and cancellation, especially during and after air raids.

Long distance journeys on passenger trains were a great test of stamina and patience. Business travellers competed for seats with crowds of service personnel moving between postings or going on leave; war workers snatching a week-end away from the factories; evacuees, adults as much as children, in continual flux... Corridors were normally jammed with passengers and their kitbags and suitcases... There were no refreshments on sale... A trip to the toilet was an expedition in itself, with an uncertain outcome.

After nightfall trains would be blacked out. Stations, too, leaving passengers to stumble about in the gloom, trying to make sense of garbled announcements over the Tannoy which were lost in the noise of whistles, shouts, slamming doors, rumbling trolleys, and the loud hiss of waiting locomotives. Waiting for what? No one seemed to know. Then the long vigils on freezing platforms for connections.... packed to the doors when, or if, they came.

All that was needed to turn the bad dream of war-time rail travel into a nightmare was for the air raid sirens to sound and a few bombs to drop down the line. Is your journey really necessary? Was it really necessary to ask?

IS YOUR JOURNEY REALLY NECESSARY?

RAILWAY EXECUTIVE COMMITTEE

49

'HOLIDAYS AT HOME'

One thing was practically certain - if your journey was for taking a holiday, then it wasn't 'really necessary' and the authorities wished to discourage it. The Minister of Health circulated local boroughs in May 1942 saying that it was desirable for workers to have a week's holiday in the summer to recuperate, but he did not want them to travel except for very short distances.

The 'Holidays At Home' idea was an attempt to deter long journeys by providing municipal entertainment locally. It was thought that if a few diversions could be arranged for children during the school summer holidays - which lasted only about three weeks in London in 1942 and 1943 - parents would be less tempted to take them farther afield.

A densely built-up area like Deptford presented special difficulties in providing for open-air events. What little public open spaces it offered had been encroached upon. Both Deptford Park and Deptford Playing Fields, for example, were taken up with shelters, allotments and barrage balloon sites. Deptford did what it could. The 1943 programme included concerts at the Lady Florence Institute, a swimming gala at Laurie Grove baths, a children's sports day at New Cross stadium, and open-air band concerts in the Memorial Gardens, Lewisham Way.

Modest and pedestrian though this programme may seem, it is doubtful whether there was anything better on offer in London's pre-war holiday haunts. Most of the seaside beaches favoured by Lewisham's and Deptford's population were covered in barbed wire and sown with mines. Some coastal towns were forbidden zones to visitors. The fun-fairs were boarded-up 'for the duration'. Nor was there fun to be had at the end of the pier - and even less in the middle, which would have been blown-up to impede invaders.

Other than that, the Germans had a nasty and well-known habit of lobbing shells across the Channel at places between Margate and

Deal. And all coastal districts had constant trouble with marauding 'tip and run' raiders. Even a place like Canterbury was not safe: it was badly blitzed in the summer and autumn of 1942.

One cannot but help suspect that these dis-incentives to travel were sufficient in themselves to keep most Deptford and Lewisham people at home for their holidays in 1942 and 1943. In the summer of 1944, of course, the question did not arise: the V1 flying bomb campaign put paid to any public entertainments local councils might have been contemplating.

DON'T MISS THE LAST BUS HOME

Local travel had its own problems and frustrations which added to the daily tribulations of doing the shopping and getting to and from work. Over 800 London buses were withdrawn from service entirely in 1940 and services were much reduced to save on fuel and manpower. Housewives were urged to travel between 10am and 4pm so as to leave more room for workers in their morning and evening scrambles for places on buses and trams.

A hundred people waiting at a bus-stop was nothing uncommon. Buses often sailed right past because they were already full to overflowing. And when one did stop, What did the bedraggled crowd hear? The distracted conductor's shout of "Full up inside, two outside", while the front of the queue tried to storm the platform.

Orderly queueing for public transport was not something you saw in pre-war days. But during the war it became established as the only way to avoid scuffles among competing forces for a scarce resource. In 1942 it was made compulsory, though an element of free-for-all survived in the case of the tramcar. This was because the queue had to break ranks and surge into the middle of the road to receive the vehicle.

In order to save on imported fuel London Transport converted some of its buses to run on coal-gas. Buses on Route 36 which ran through the borough to Hither Green station were among those converted.

Children's concert, Telegraph Hill, September 1943. Such 'do-it-yourself' entertainments were intended to encourage people to avoid travelling for their holidays.

Special express bus on route 47 which ran through Deptford and Lewisham to Bromley Garage during the Blitz when rail services were put out of action.

To save on petrol some buses ran on coal-gas produced by an anthracite-burning trailer.

They towed an anthracite burner that looked like a large oil drum on two wheels and which had to be re-fuelled every 80 miles. The contraption did not take too kindly to hills. Progress for the 36 bus and its smoky trailer in the climb up Sandhurst Road to Torridon Road library tended to be an asthmatic and arthritic struggle against gravity.

Not least among the inconveniences of war-time travel was the fact that there were no buses on the roads after 10.30pm, except for a few stragglers 'running in' to their garages. 'Catching the last bus (or train) home' was a major constraint on an evening out. There were no taxis to be hired at that time of night, nor could a lift be had in a friend's car - he did not have a car; or if he did, he was allowed no petrol for it. Like most of London, Lewisham simply closed down for the night at 10.30. The blacked-out streets emptied of all life. Nothing stirred until dawn.... Unless an air raid occurred.

The windows of London buses and tube trains were covered by sticky, green anti-blast netting with just a small diamond shape left for passengers to see through. This was done to prevent injury from flying splinters in a bomb blast. People who made attempts to unstick the material were rebuked in verse by 'Billy Brown of London Town', a cartoon figure in striped trousers and bowler hat specially created by London Transport to advise travellers on travel matters.

"I trust you'll pardon my correction,

That stuff is there for your protection."

Which invited the response:

"We thank you for your information,

We want to see the bloody station."

One particular journey I remember was from Cardiff and the train had to stop outside Reading for some considerable time owing to a raid in London. When it finally started, it went very slowly with many stops. The railways were of course a target for bombers. Finally we reached Paddington and in the Underground there was the familiar sight of people settled in for the night's shelter. I felt an intruder, but the trains did not seem to disturb them.

When I got to Charing Cross there were no more trains to Charlton, so I got as far as New Cross where I hoped to get a tram. Whilst waiting at the stop, a van driver offered me a lift which I gratefully accepted. There was no fear of attack in those days and men were protective. He took me right to the door. He was probably as glad of some company as I was, and got me home nice and quickly. Most journeys in those days were accompanied by the unexpected, not always pleasant but never boring.

Edie McHardy

Millions Like Us
[Title of a 1943 British film about women factory workers]

There were, indeed, millions of women conscripted ('directed' was the word they used) into armaments and munitions factories across the country. By the end of 1942 some 8 ½ million women, aged 19-46, had been obliged to register for some form of national service. The labour supply became so stretched to meet the demands of the war that in July 1943 women up to the age of 51 had to register.

National service included, of course, military service, but much the larger proportion of women were employed in war-work. This was usually taken to mean work in factories engaged in war-production. However, any employment helpful to the prosecution of the war was, in a sense, 'war-work'.

The only kinds of occupation which might keep a woman out of the clutches of heavy industry included, obviously enough, farming - as served by the Women's Land Army - an arduous physical life for which not everyone was suited. Other jobs included nursing, teaching (though for this it helped if you were also middle-aged), full-time Civil Defence, and possibly bus-conducting (the 'clippies'), though the Ministry of Labour rather favoured this as a part-time job for women with domestic responsibilities.

Applications for exemption from war-work were generally treated on their individual merits, but jobs like shop assistants, waitresses, hairdressers, typists, barmaids, to name a few, were unlikely to get a woman exemption, unless she had genuine family dependents, or a physical disability, or some other convincing reason for staying put.

Land girls go off to the Farm.

54

Thousands of women were sent to work in munitions factories.

For women in Deptford and Lewisham, direction into war-work often meant they were sent to another part of the country, a more industrial part, where they were found 'digs' or joined a communal hostel with others in the same boat. A young woman from the suburbs, separated from her family for the first time, was bound to be homesick when deposited in a strange and uninviting land of smoking chimney-stacks, cold grey streets and drizzly skies in the bleakness of war-austerity.

Factory hours were long and tedious, amid the roar of machinery and the smell of machine oil. Standing all day (or all night, for factories worked in shifts around-the-clock), tapping, drilling, filing, milling, reaming.... making a 'thingy-me-jig', a sprocket or a socket, that was 'going to win the war' - if only she knew, or cared, what it was for or what it was supposed to do. Her job was just to make it. The less one knew, the less one could reveal by 'careless talk'.

Young women seemed better able to 'switch off' in repetitive work and to think of brighter things without impairing the quality of their output. The authorities, for their part, tried to relieve the strain and monotony. BBC broadcasts of 'Music While You Work' and 'Workers Playtime' were relayed each working day over factory loudspeakers. In literally thousands of factories all over the country ENSA parties (Entertainments National Services Association) came to give lunchtime concerts in works canteens.

It was a raw and rough life for those far from home and unaccustomed to industrial work at the sharp end, and they needed all the moral support they could get. Some local women were luckier inasmuch as they found work within travelling distance of home - at the Woolwich Arsenal, or at Siemens Brothers in Charlton, or Elliott Brothers in Lewisham, for example. Yet every manufacturing company became involved in war-production. Firms were glad to assist in the great drive to victory. There was only one customer now - the government.

The list of plants and workshops operating on war production in Lewisham and Deptford could be extended almost indefinitely. The 'Leeway' works in Lee High Road switched its considerable manufacturing capacity from baby carriages, push chairs, pedal cars and children's scooters to 'metal bashing' for the military in a big

A Temporary Civil Servant

The Civil Service - I was asked if that would suit me. I didn't wish to go into the services if I could help it because it meant leaving the family and they did rather depend on me in many ways. So I said I would do that and I went to the Board of Trade. It was a wartime department, export licensing, which meant that all goods leaving this country, being exported, had to have a licence. Some were rejected. The licences were pretty tight to come by. I went into the dangerous drugs section. I had to learn all decimalisation, weights and everything. Not so much the money side, I didn't have to worry so much about that. But I did have to know about weights and quite a lot about the various names of drugs. It was pretty uphill because it was all strange and fresh to me.

I knew that we were not what was known as 'permanent civil servants.' We were only there as conscripts. We knew that if we were fortunate - there was a lot of wangling always went on, no matter what it was, in promotions and all sorts of things - you felt that you might be given the chance to become a permanent civil servant or your job would end and you would have to go and look in other quarters for a job. What I didn't like was that if you asked to become a permanent

WOMEN OF BRITAIN

COME INTO
THE FACTORIES

Wray Optical Works, *Downham made lenses for reconnaissance aircraft cameras and designed a telephoto lens for the RAF which was said to be far superior to any in use by Germany.*

Holmes Plating Co., *Blackheath was put on round-the-clock work in the vital task of plating aircraft and radar parts.*

Elliott Brothers, *Lewisham engaged all its resources completely and wholeheartedly to the war effort, including the manufacture of naval gunfire control equipment and electrical instruments for the RAF.*

Clover Leaf Ltd., *Ladywell mass-produced gaskets on contract to the Ministry of Supply.*

S.W. Farmer & Son, *Lewisham was engaged in ceaseless production, round-the-clock, seven-days-a-week, turning-out Bailey Bridges for the Allied armies.*

Lewisham Engineering Co., *Lewisham produced bayonets, components for tank-landing craft, and Diesel engine pumps.*

Gardiner & Gulland Ltd., *Hither Green, makers of catering equipment (which was still needed for the armed forces and in factory canteens) added various war appliances to their range, for example, aircraft petrol tanks. Production lines operated day and night without pause.*

B. Kimber, Allen & Co., *Lewisham produced gun sights and millions of cable accessories for the Navy.*

way. Aerograph Limited at Lower Sydenham, makers of spray guns, turned to more lethal weapons. Food Factories, such as Chiltonian at Lee and Robertson's 'Golden Shred' works at Bellingham, saw much of their output go to the forces.

An outstanding contribution to the war's success was that of Molins in Deptford, famous for their cigarette-making machines. The firm invented and produced an automatic fuze-setter for the 3.7 inch anti-aircraft gun which was responsible for the incredible rate of fire ultimately achieved by Britain's AA defences. The firm also invented and made a fast-firing six-pounder gun for the Mosquito fighter-bomber, dubbed the 'Molins gun'. These and other new devices brought unstinted praise from army and RAF top-brass, and from Lord Beaverbrook, when Minister of Aircraft Production.

Harry S. Truman, US President, awarded Desmond Molins, Vice-President of the firm, the Medal of Freedom, with Bronze Palm, for contributing "immeasurably to the success of the Allied war effort." Mr Molins said the honour belonged to the firm, and it is hardly necessary to add that women war workers figured strongly in that success.

Come and help with the VICTORY HARVEST

You are needed in the fields !

APPLY TO NEAREST EMPLOYMENT EXCHANGE FOR LEAFLET & ENROLMENT FORM OR WRITE DIRECT TO THE DEPARTMENT OF AGRICULTURE FOR SCOTLAND 15 GROSVENOR STREET, EDINBURGH.

civil servant you had to give up all your promotions, the privileges or anything which your promotions gave you, plus your salary, and start from the very basic. Because before the war it was a long process to be accepted as a permanent civil servant. But because of war service they were quite willing to waive some of that. But - it was all I suppose a matter of pride, which is only natural - why should you go to the bottom on the lowest salary, and you knew that your chances of promotion out of that category were very small because there were lots of other people. They wouldn't require so many staff for one thing. Departments would actually close down and it would all get back to the smug little circle it had been before the war. I didn't like that. I resented it, because I had worked very hard, as we all had in the Service during the war. It was compulsory 52 hours a week which is quite a long week. And we did extra work as well, weekends and so on. I felt that we had given a lot to the Service for which we were not paid, which is only a natural thing to think, and you thought "Well, why have I got to be humiliated and go to the very bottom?" It was pride - you felt you'd done your duty and you'd done it to the best of your ability, and you didn't quite fancy going right down to the bottom. I later

learned that those people who did accept, and accepted Grade Three, which was the lowest form of life in the Civil Service, never got out of it, and they were never allowed to forget that they had been conscripts during the war. Very unpleasant.

Miss Applegate

Repaired Steamrollers For The Invasion

I was looking after all the big lorries, the dust lorries and all that kind of thing, repairing them you know and keeping them on the road and then the Manpower board sent for me and they made me go and work at Aveling-Barfords at Sydenham. It was because they was going round and taking all the rollers - petrol rollers, diesel rollers and steam rollers all from different councils and they was sending them to us for repair, getting ready for the invasion, and I was up there for about two years I suppose.

Jim Jeal

Resented Working With Women At First

Things were much stricter before the war. There was no such thing before the war as Christian names. Christian names weren't used. That never came about till during the war. Also the grocery shops had no women working with them, they were all male staff. They were all women during the war nearly. First of all I was very resentful of it, very resentful of it. I don't know why but I was. I'd got used to the company of men I suppose, and then suddenly having women work beside you, and no other man around anywhere. I was not the only one, but there were only two of us in the shop and about a dozen women.

Eventually it changed to enjoying working with them. They was all so jolly. Mind you, they weren't youngsters all of them. One or two, but most of them had to go in the services or on more essential work, so I had women working with me whose sons were in the army. But they were all very jolly and they used to sing and get on with their work and have a bit of fun during the day.

Mr Drury snr

If *you* can't go to the factory help the neighbour who *can*

How you can help

Arrange **now** with a neighbour to look after her children when she goes to her war-work—or give your name to

CARING FOR WAR WORKERS' CHILDREN IS A NATIONAL SERVICE

Issued by the Ministry of Health

Trained As A Nurse, Sent Into Munitions

I had to do this job in the Arsenal. My mother said to me that in the First World War she had had to work in the danger building and she said, "Don't let them put you in there because you get yellow skin." The cordite. You get a blood condition. She said "Whatever you do, fight them about that," so I said to the girl in the office, "I'm not going in the danger building." She said, "If you don't you'll have to go to prison. So I said, "Well, I'm sorry, I'll go to prison". I am not going into the danger building. My mother worked there and I've seen how it affected her and I will not work in the danger building." So I said, "Why can't I do something like looking after children or nursing people as I've been used to doing?" I trained for a nurse for a while you see, years before this. Anyway, they said, "No. You've got to work in the Arsenal. You've got to go." So I said, "I'm not going, so you can do as you like" and I walked out. Anyway, they let me know that I could go into building E36 which was right next door to the danger building!

Working In The Woolwich Arsenal

I was examining 303's - rifle bullets. We had to examine all these things. What you had to do is pick up a handful of bullets, about a dozen and you held them in your hand and you shook them up like that and then you rolled them backwards and forwards like that - you had to examine every one of those dozen and not a pin prick must show. You had to examine a dozen at a time to get your work through. And then when you'd finished doing that you bunched them up and you examined all the heads carefully right the way round, very very carefully because a little pin prick on there could make a rifle kick back and blow a man's shoulder out, I was told. So it used to worry me to death - "I mustn't miss one". Then you had to turn them up and examine the bullet end. They mustn't have a dent or a scratch or a pin prick in them. Woe betide you if they went to the finals and they found a pin prick on your box. The brass casing of the bullet had to be absolutely smooth. They were 303's. They were nasty little things.

Susan Swann

Queueing For The One-And-Nines

More than any other relaxation, with the possible exception of the radio (the 'wireless', one should say), cinemagoing kept the nation's spirits up when the outlook was at its darkest. The success of films in easing the burdens of fear and loneliness, discomfort and weariness, owed more to Hollywood than to British studios. People wanted movement, colour, music, comedy.... to escape from the realities of war, rather than to be reminded of them.

War films and documentary-style productions were not well-liked generally, and too many British films fell into these categories. Hollywood offered glamour and romance... escapism. Its war films had the same sort of far-off, make-believe quality about them. British war films were just a little too close to home for real comfort. Which is not to say British films did not fill the cinemas. Cinemas filled up whatever was shown. It was more a matter of what made the audiences feel good and what made them feel slightly uncomfortable.

Programmes were shown continuously and, because it was usual in the evenings to wait in long queues for seats to become vacant, it seldom happened that cinemagoers caught the programme at the beginning. When the programme came back to a familiar scene, they rose reluctantly, saying with disappointment, "This is where we came in."

The queues would still be there when they came out - unless the last showing of the day was well-advanced. The most popular seats were the rear-stalls costing one shilling and ninepence (about 8 ½p). "Queueing for the one-and-nines", the commissionaire cried. Your best chance of getting a seat without an interminable wait was to splash out two-and-ninepence, possibly as much as three-and-sixpence, for the circle. It was too great an extravagance for most pockets.

When the Blitz started, 'Gaslight' with Anton Walbrook was showing at the Gaumont, Lewisham, and Arthur Askey in 'Charley's Aunt' at the Queen's Hall, Rushey Green. But the continual bombing forced many cinemas to close down. Within days the Savoy, Lee Green announced it was 'Temporarily Closed'; the Prince of Wales, Lewisham said 'Closed Until Further Notice'; the State, Sydenham simply put up the shutters. Yet air raids could not counter the attractions of the silver screen for long. By the end of 1940 all Lewisham's cinemas were back in business, apart from those "permanently gone", as the security-conscious Lewisham Borough News euphemistically expressed it.

It was the practice of managements to display a slide on the screen when an air raid started which invited patrons to leave and take shelter if they wished. What else would you expect in the middle of 'Target For Tonight' or 'Dangerous Moonlight'? The show went on regardless, so you didn't get your money back if you followed the advice.

The V1 flying bombs in 1944 affected cinema attendances worst. This was because they came over at all times of the day and night. "It took nerve of a peculiar order to sit still in your seat and enjoy a film while the regular chug-chug of the engine drew nearer and then stopped, apparently right over the theatre." (Guy Morgan, 'Red Roses Every Night')

Ballroom Dancing was one of the war's main relaxations, though this dance in the hall of Aske's Girls School (September 1941) has yet to warm up. Meanwhile the men are 'Wallflowers' and the women have a dance with each other.

Left: The re-opening of the Lewisham Hippodrome two years after being damaged in the Blitz.

VARIETY WAS THE SPICE OF LIFE

Lewisham and Deptford each boasted a major variety theatre - the Lewisham Hippodrome in Rushey Green, Catford, and the New Cross Empire. Both offered live programmes of the country's leading performers to large and eager audiences. They saw the New Year in with style in 1940. At the New Cross Empire there was Tommy Trinder and Turner Layton, while 'Cinderella', with Ernie Lotinga, at the Hippodrome was followed by 'Variety's Welcome to 1940' with Ronald Frankau and the comedy duo, Clapham and Dwyer.

Britain's first war-time broadcast variety show came from the Lewisham Hippodrome on 15 February 1940, starring Suzette Tarri, Wheeler and Wilson, and Sid Millward and His Nitwits. Unfortunately, the theatre got its timing wrong with the revue, 'All Right on the Western Front' on May 1940. It was performed during the week when everything started to go badly wrong in France. Goodness knows how misplaced some of the jokes and songs may have turned out to be.

Live theatre by its nature suffered badly during periods of intense air raids. The first night of the Blitz found Adelaide Hall at the Hippodrome doing extra 'turns' through the night to an audience which was unable to get home. At the New Cross Empire they played records to an audience similarly trapped. The next week's programmes never took place. The Western Brothers, Dick Henderson, and Harry Tate, jnr., were to appear, but continuing bombing put paid to it. The Hippodrome remained closed until September 1942, having sustained serious damage early on in the Blitz.

DOING THE PALAIS GLIDE

The popularity of dance music came to greater prominence as war conditions loosened some of the constraints which parents imposed on their adolescent children, especially the girls. 75 per cent of Londoners reported that they enjoyed dance music - a social fact not publicly known hitherto.

Dance halls boomed in the war years, especially after they were licensed till 11pm or later. It was not just the music, nor the dancing for that matter. Attending the local 'hop' was the best way available for young people to meet members of the opposite sex in a relaxed, informal atmosphere. That's what worried their parents.

New Cross Palais de Danse was south east London's leading dance venue, and it did not operate a ban on the modern 'hot' styles from America, as was the case in some places in deference to middle-age tastes. In 1940 a Brockley girl died at the New Cross Palais after falling down while doing the latest American craze, the Jitterbug. A young man demonstrated the movements of this "American innovation" at the inquest for the edification of the Ladywell Coroner, who described it as "peculiar and very vulgar".

The EMPIRE, NEW CROSS
LONDON. S.E.14.

Managing Directors: R. H. GILLESPIE & GEORGE BLACK

Direction : GEORGE BLACK

ALL STAR VARIETY
STAGE ∴ OF
FILM ∴ B.B.C. ARTISTES

PROGRAMME

Sunday, November 2nd, 1941
in aid of
The Rescue Service Benevolent Funds

In the Metropolitan Boroughs of
Lewisham, Greenwich, Deptford, Woolwich and Bermondsey
organized by
LEADER C. F. LESTER (Lewisham Rescue Service)
under the auspices of
LEWISHAM RESCUE SERVICE BENEVOLENT FUND

Resident Manager ... ... EDWARD P. DURHAM
Director of Music ... ... KEVIN MALLON
Stage Manager ... ... JIMMY BLISS

In accordance with the requirements of the London County Council:—
1. The public may leave at the end of the performance or exhibition by all exit or entrance doors, and such doors must at that time be open.
2. All gangways, corridors, staircases and external passageways intended for exit shall be kept entirely free from obstruction, whether permanent or temporary.
3. Persons shall not be permitted to stand or sit in any of the gangways intersecting the seating, or to sit in any of the other gangways. If standing be permitted in the gangways at the sides and rear of the seating, sufficient space shall be left for persons to pass easily to and fro and to have free access to exits.
4. The safety curtain must be lowered and raised in the presence of each audience.

"When They Sound The Last All-Clear"

No symbol of the war's ending for people on the Home Front could have better expressed their longing than the sounding of the last All Clear. No sound was more welcome in the Blitz and in subsequent raids - that steady, resonant note of the sirens announcing the end of one more attack. It would have made a fitting and dramatic signal at the end of the war in Europe, especially if followed by two minutes silence of thanks and remembrance nation-wide. 11am would have been the right timing for it, as on Armistice Day. (It was about this time on Sunday, 3 September 1939 that the first war-time sounding of the 'warning' was heard). But it was not to be.

People did hear the last All Clear, of course. Only they had no way of telling that it was the last one, so it had no special meaning or significance. For Deptford and Lewisham it was heard at 7.58am, 28 March 1945, a moment or two after London's final V1 flying bomb came to ground in Chislehurst. Just hours before that the last V2 rocket of the war landed in Orpington. Again, people had no way of telling that it was the last of these pitiless missiles until several weeks had passed.

COUNTDOWN TO PEACE

Wednesday, 2 May 1945 was in its way the most important milestone at home in the count-down towards Peace. Announcements on this date amounted to an official acknowledgement that London's long ordeal was finally over:

Families Had To Adjust

In early July, my husband was admitted to the army hospital near Maidstone. I visited with my two year old daughter. Later on, he was allowed to come home for a day - I recall him arriving in his 'Hospital Blues'. He was discharged from Barming in August and sent home until the necessary documentation was completed, finally being 'invalided out' of the army after five years service with a 20% disability pension. He attended Olympia in October to receive his discharge papers, demob suit etc, and a gratuity of £74. He had to re-adjust to civilian life - and the life of a married man with a wife and child. I had to adjust to having a husband now permanently at home.

My daughter now aged two and a quarter years had to adjust to this new set of circumstances. She had been used to this father in uniform, putting in an occasional appearance on leaves. Now there was this father no longer in uniform - and here all of the time. Up to then, I had been the sole person in her life - it must have been puzzling for her. It is only with hindsight that one is able to assess the situation. My husband was

- **The national air raid warning system discontinued as from noon.**

The warning operated 1,226 times in London. 2,193 hours and 35 minutes were spent 'under alert'; one hour for every day of the war. It would have been more had there been warnings for every raid and for all the V1s and V2s.

- **All public air raid shelters to be closed.**

- **Civil Defence organisation and Royal Observer Corps to be disbanded.**

An Order of the Day from Mr Herbert Morrison (Minister of Home Security) expressed deep gratitude for all they had done. Deptford Council added its own "keen appreciation and profound admiration" of the splendid services given at all times during the conflict.

- **Official return of London evacuees to commence at end of month.**

500,000 mothers and children were expected to return under the official scheme. Only 10 per cent of the number actually waited that long to come home.

So it was plain to all that the conflict in Europe was reaching its final climax. It could only be a matter of days.... The air of expectancy and excitement began to be felt everywhere.

There had been still earlier portents. Months before, in November 1944, the Home Guard was stood down. A final march-past was held in Hyde Park on 3 December, at which the King took the salute. It was all over: The guarding of the country's vital installations, the road blocks and hand-to-hand combat, church parades on Sunday.... Dad handed in his rifle, wondering whether it had all been a bad dream. In September 1944 a modified form of street lighting, known as the 'Dim Out', was permitted. It was more depressing in some ways than not seeing the streets at all. Deptford's Dim Out consisted

conscripted in April 1940 at the age of twenty-three. Up until then, he had lived with his parents, with no responsibility for the domestic issues. In the army he was fed and watered, so had no worries in that field. Of course it was not an easy life - stresses and strains and physical drains on emotions were present. He was made a sergeant in 1941, so had to be responsible for men under him, some of them older than himself, and sergeants were often in a position where the "buck stopped with them".

Then catapulted back into civilian life in an entirely new set of circumstances. Not really aware of what his role was - what he was responsible for, expecting there would be little difference in his life. I had to adjust to having another person to care for - and my routine to be altered considerably. There were hundreds of people like us.

Margaret Kippin

precisely of 144 gas lights and 69 electric lights in the borough's main roads. The Dim Out itself was lifted on 23 April 1945, except in a five-mile coastal belt, thus ending 2,061 nights of Black Out in one form or another. Yet London households at first found it hard to break the habit - only one window in ten appeared to be lighted - and it was another three months before street lighting could be fully restored.

The last winter of war also witnessed the removal of emergency water tanks from bomb sites; the erection of pre-fabricated homes (pre-fabs) in their place; and the continuing repairs to a million damaged homes in London, with the help of thousands of building workers from Scotland, Wales and the provinces - while rockets were falling and undoing the good work.

VICTORY IN EUROPE

Yes, it was all happening, as the modern saying goes; this gradual unwinding of the Home Front. Then on Monday, 7 May came the long-awaited message that Germany had surrendered unconditionally and that Tuesday would be Victory-in-Europe Day and a public holiday. The revelling did not wait upon the morrow. Huge crowds gathered in the West End on the Monday evening. On VE-Day itself tremendous scenes of rejoicing swept central London. Vast multitudes gathered outside Buckingham Palace and in Whitehall. The crowds danced, sang, drank, lit bonfires, let off fireworks, waved flags, climbed lamp posts and famous monuments, and they cheered themselves hoarse.

That's the West End for you, always larger than life. In Deptford and Lewisham the celebrations were generally more subdued, but none the less enjoyable for that. Street parties for the children were held in many working class turnings. Special entertainments and amateur shows were laid on. In hundreds of pubs impromptu sing-songs and 'knees-ups' went on into the night in a haze of tobacco smoke and the

A Few Days Later You Came Down To Earth

You'd felt really happy that everyone would be coming home from the forces and there'd be no more bombing, but a few days later you came down to earth and you realised that life was never going to be the same again. That things had completely changed, your whole life. You'd been through the whole war. What I kept thinking was, "It's never going to end". You knew it must end, it couldn't go on for ever. But I kept thinking, "It's never going to end. The bombing is never going to end. People never going to stop being injured." I was so happy when they actually said, "It's over," but a few days later we then started thinking, "What's life going to be like now?"

Lil Murrell

Right: The King and Queen on their victory tour of south London seen passing destroyed shops in the centre of Lewisham.

A Great Sense of Relief

I was trying to finish a rather important lot of work. Somebody rushed in the office and said, "It's over! It's over! Come on - Put that down!" I said, "No. I'm finishing my work. You're telling me that the war is over? Well, one expected that. That's alright." And I continued with my work until I'd finished it. That was me, the way I liked things. You didn't go riotously joyful or anything. You came home and enjoyed it with your family and you just breathed a big sigh of relief that there would be no more bombing raids and no more lives lost - as you thought then - of course there have been so many other incidents since, in one shape or another. You felt a great sense of relief that you could hope and that you could plan a better life, not realising that life was never going to be quite the same as it had been before the war. But we did - we had to do it. There were parties and wonderful homecomings for the troops. There was sadness because of those that didn't come come, service people that didn't return. It was very mixed really. I don't think I ever felt over-jubilant because there was the memory of the things that had happened, people that were no longer there. But some people did go over the moon. That was up to the individual, how they felt.

Miss Applegate

The Crowds Were Totally United In Happiness

I had journeyed home to Catford Bridge Station as usual, and there met a girl friend with whom I had previously arranged to go to the cinema straight from work. Together we walked down into Catford and then into the Plaza cinema (now known as the Cannon). Imagine our surprise and amazement when we made our exit to find both my parents and younger brother waiting for us. "Come on girl, get a move on," said my father. "We're all going up to town." "Whatever for?". "To join the crowds to celebrate," he replied. So, back we all went to Catford Bridge Station, boarded the first train and alighted at Charing Cross to find crowds of people all milling about.

The air of excitement was unbelievable. "Where are we going now?" I asked my father. "Up the Mall and along to the Palace," he replied. There must have been thousands of us merrily wending our way through Admiralty Arch and into the Mall. There were bonfires everywhere, throwing flames into the air and lighting our way. After all the years of blackout and blue lightbulbs, it was truly glorious to be able to have light around us which was of our own making.

whiff of stale beer. Churches throughout the boroughs held thanksgiving services which were attended by civic figures and other community leaders.

For all the public display, it may be assumed that a majority of people stayed quietly at home, listening to events on the wireless, enjoying a glass of beer or sherry, reading a book.... For them it was enough that the news from Europe was so good. It made them happy. But they were not the sort to 'make a song and dance' about it.

For many people victory in Europe was an occasion for mixed feelings - all those who had suffered personal loss or permanent injury in the long conflict. They were grateful that it was over, but could the scenes of revelry do other than make more poignant the pain they felt? There were the tragic evacuees whose parents had been killed in the bombing, and others whose miserable fate it was to be abandoned by their parents while they were absent from home.

Some believed, and they were right in a way, that the celebrations were premature. Millions of service personnel were absent from the party, scattered across several continents and all the oceans. Many of these absent fathers, sons, and husbands remained locked in bloody combat in farthest Asia. Others faced disease, brutality and starvation as prisoners of war. No early end to the war in the Far East was in sight, so far as ordinary people could tell. In the event, Japan accepted unconditional surrender on 14 August 1945 and VJ-Day was celebrated on the following day in much the same way as VE-Day.

PEACE WAS PAINFUL, TOO

One thing which peace did not bring was the end to rationing and to shortages of all kinds. They got worse in many ways. It was not until nearly a decade later that Britain finally rid itself of this legacy of the war and entered upon an age of unparalleled material prosperity. The physical scars of the bombing in Deptford and Lewisham took still longer to heal. Like the desolation in Lewisham's shopping centre,

On and on up the Mall we walked, so closely packed and excited that we felt totally united in our happiness. Finally we reached the area around the Victoria and Albert memorial, which was already covered with people who had climbed up and around it for a better view of the Palace. Slowly a chant grew louder, "We want the King!" until it became a roar, and then the tall doors on the balcony finally opened and the royal family came into view. The cheers that welcomed their appearance must have been heard miles away.

Lena Richardson

I Cried Myself To Sleep

In the early days of the war we used to talk of what we would do when it all ended. I remember my aunt used to say when she brought in the early morning cup of tea - "One day nearer, Peg". But a lot of water had gone under the bridge since those days. Now I was older and perhaps wiser.

I have memories of feeling numb - no feeling of euphoria. Three months previously a dear and valued friend, who was also my daughter's godfather, had been shot down on a bombing raid and we had only recently received confirmation. Earlier in the war my young brother had been

these remained for many years as silent reminders that 'war had passed this way'.

Just as the coming of war called for tremendous personal adjustments, so, no less, did the return of peace. It was not a matter of going back and carrying on from where you left off. Where you left off could not be re-created. Too much had changed. You had changed. Fathers returned who were complete strangers, not always welcome strangers, to their children. Wives had achieved a new independence. Returning servicemen found that their old jobs had been taken in their absence by people who had remained civilians throughout the war. Others simply could not settle into the old routine of their pre-war jobs.

Peace was not easy. The transition from war to peace was harder yet. The war made an indelible imprint on the lives of those who experienced it at first-hand. It seeped into the very marrow of their existence. That's what made peace so hard for so many. Now, fifty years on, they say the war has become solely a matter of history. But that it can never be, not so long as a single survivor is alive to remember it.

Rokeby Road, Brockley celebrates VE-Day

killed in a similar way - and so many of the boys from the church would not be coming home. I could not help remembering them. I recall feeling somewhat like a robot as I completed my household chores - and had the hope that someone from the family would come over (they were living in Clapham at the time). No telephones to be able to ring up and chat about it. It was all so quiet everywhere - the house- the road. Only the elderly widower in the basement. I remember sitting by the window with my twenty month old daughter on my lap. I recall how - in the early days of the Blitz, going for a walk by myself and thinking - the world - and life as we knew it - had gone for good, and despite the fact that one was grateful that at least in the European war there was no threat of danger - This feeling I had had in the Blitz reinforced. I went to bed that night - early - and must confess - cried myself to sleep!

Margaret Kippin

Down to the village pub on VE-Day....

One day there was great excitement. The War was over, it was VE day, and people were singing and dancing in the streets all over the land, while great crowds flocked to Trafalgar Square, and everyone had a high old time. So what did I do? I got up early as usual, milked and mucked out the cows, put the churns out to be collected and fed the other animals, there being no-one else to do it! My landlady's husband helped with the afternoon milking so I would be finished early, then we all wend down to the village pub for a party. I didn't feel wildly excited being the only stranger in this small community, although I must say I was generously included in everything, but I wanted to be with my own family and friends, although I knew this wasn't possible. Most of all I wanted to be able to get to Trafalger Square and join in the excitement with all the other Londonders. However we all had a happy evening in and around the pub, and the following day went back to work, at least those that were capable did!

Left the Land Army and went home....

I went on working in my temporary job until I had a letter from H.Q. telling me I was being replaced by a permanent girl, the farmer having decided not to have the cowman back, so I returned to the Hostel where I was stationed.

However, it was not the same. While I had been away, a lot of girls had returned home, our very dear Matron had become ill and had been retired, and there seemed very little purpose in anything any more. We went on working on the land until some time near the end of Harvesting (after the end of the War in Japan, which seemed to fizzle out quietly with little excitement), when I fainted one day, fortunately on the ground after having just come down a ladder from the top of a stack! The doctor told me it was time I went home, as I'd done enough farm work, so I was released from the Land Army and went home for a rest before looking for a job.

Things were not the same....

I can remember feeling very bitter at this time. A lot of young men I'd known had died. My sister and many friends had married and moved away, and I was living at home with my parents and much younger brother, with whom at that time I had little in common. Also, I received nothing from the Land Army except a few clothing coupons, whereas other women's services were fully equipped upon release and also received a certain amount of money. I was in an awful predicament because none of my civilian clothes fitted me! Although I hadn't put on much weight, I had become fitter and more muscular because of the heavy work, so there was a lot of pinching, scraping and begging of coupons from various people, mainly by my mother, who was marvellous!

Inside there was an empty space....

Although the War was over, food and clothing was still rationed, and a vast amount of bomb damage had not been cleared away. Everything was in short supply so an army of 'spivs' sprang up, able to get anything for anyone, at a price of course, and usually illegally. People were exhausted and had little enthusiasm for anything much, and although all were pleased that the War was actually over, somehow it seemed to leave an empty space. We didn't quite know what to do with ourselves! After being geared up for six years not only to survive but also to win the War, now having won it, what were we going to do with it?

Dorothy Barton
(Women's Land Army)

Albert Dolphin *(posthumous George Cross)*, from Boyland Road, Downham, who sacrificed his life to save that of an injured nurse at the South Eastern Hospital by throwing himself across her when a roof collapsed.

Bernard Bennie *(George Medal)*, a member of Lewisham rescue squad, who searched all-night while bombing was in progress for buried victims at Engleheart Road, Catford, though suffering from burns and electric shock and twice overcome by gas fumes. Was himself removed to hospital.

Albert Brittan *(George Medal)*, a rescue worker from Milton Court Road, Deptford, who tunnelled for five hours under debris during an all-night raid to rescue a baby and three adults. He was himself trapped when a house-roof collapsed but continued to direct the operation.

Albert Clarke *(George Medal)* Auxiliary fireman from Bellingham. Though off-duty he worked for two hours under a demolished house in Moremead Road to extricate a trapped woman, ignoring a powerful concentration of escaping gas in the narrow space which threatened both their lives.

Frederick Curtis *(BEM)* AFS Section Officer. Was in charge of a team at a fire in Ilderton Road when he was knocked unconscious by a bomb blast. On recovering consciousness he insisted on resuming command of the firefighting and showed outstanding leadership.

J.W. Donno *(George Medal)*, Lewisham rescue squad. He rescued five people from devastated homes in Ladywell Park, during which time he was twice buried in the ruins. He was removed to hospital unconscious after being struck by falling debris.

Mary Fleming and Aileen Turner *(George Medals)*, nurses at Grove Park Hospital. When the hospital received a direct hit they climbed up through the upper windows and crawled on their stomachs across a swaying floor in complete darkness to lead trapped patients to safety. Shortly afterwards the floor collapsed into the ward below. A third nurse, **Ruby Rosser,** won the GM for shielding a patient from falling debris with her own body. She then helped the patient to safety just before the floor above crashed into the ward.

John Foley *(George Medal)*, stoker at the Park Hospital, Hither Green. He saved an injured nurse from being burned to death by climbing into the flames without regard for his own life and carrying her to safety.

Pol. Sgt. D. Grigg *(George Medal)* of 'P' Division, Catford, who removed unexploded bombs by hand from a crashed Heinkel bomber at Bromley Common, where injured people were trapped under the wreckage, and carried them across the A.21 main road to open ground.

Joseph Hoyle *(George Medal)*, rescue worker. During heavy bombing he laboured through the night after his period of duty had expired to rescue injured victims in the basement ruins of the Central Hall, Deptford.

Peter Inglis *(George Medal)*, Deptford rescue service. He rescued a number of people after tunnelling through two wrecked and gas-filled basements in extremely hazardous conditions.

Dr H.S. Knight *(OBE),* in charge of Deptford's mobile casualty unit in 1944-1945. The award was in recognition of his outstanding devotion to duty and indefatigable leadership in the treatment of hundreds of injured at all the major V2 incidents in the area.

Tommy Lloyd *(King's Commendation).* Aged 14, he burrowed out of the bombed basement of his home in Deptford and assisted his sisters to safety through the route he had made. He helped rescue workers to find his buried mother and to retrieve her body.

Harold Reed *(OBE)*, Deptford Town Clerk. Despite suffering serious facial wounds from flying splinters during the Blitz from which he never fully recovered, he continued with the onerous duties of his office until the war was over.

Annie Wilkins *(BEM)* of Cressingham Road, Lewisham, and **Bessie Wulbern** *(BEM)*, Auxiliary firewomen. They stayed on alone at the AFS sub-station in Bush Road, Bermondsey after it had been set alight by incendiary bombs and continued to relay messages and direct fire crews to where they were needed. When ordered to leave they thumbed a lift to Deptford fire station, where they attended blinded and burned firemen who were laid out on the floor awaiting ambulances.

Joseph Wood *(OBE)*, Downham rescue worker, who risked his life by crawling under destroyed houses in Downham Way to give drink and encouragement to trapped young children, and later helped to bring them out.

The Royal Victory motorcade mobbed by waiting crowds among the ruins of Lewisham High Street. The scene is a moving reminder of the cost of that victory

Left: Victory party on the green, Athelney Street, Bellingham

Right: Street party, Wildfell Road, off Rushey Green, Catford

How we went to war is published by the London Borough of Lewisham to commemorate the sacrifices made by the people of Deptford and Lewisham during the Second World War, and to tell their story of that dramatic and tragic time, both in their own words and in the more 'factual' style of the local historian, Lewis Blake. The publication, which marks the 50th anniversary of the ending of the war in 1945, is the first to provide an overall view of how the war was experienced in this corner of London. It is hoped that as well as serving as a fitting tribute to a previous generation of residents, it will provide a better understanding among younger people - especially schoolchildren - of what life was like in the local community between 1939 and 1945.

Sincere thanks are due to those individuals who gave up their time to record personal reminiscences of the war years, and to Pam Schweizer and Rib Davis of the Age Exchange Reminiscence Centre for collecting and transcribing these recollections. For reasons of space it has not been possible to include all this material in the book, but whether included or not every reminiscence has been gratefully received, and thanks are extended to all who participated in the project.

Most of the photographs have come from the collection in the Lewisham Local Studies Centre, where John Coulter made the necessary arrangements for providing a good cross-section of pictures. Others have come from the Imperial War Museum and from various private people, who have kindly given permission for their use. The design and layout of the book is by Keith Crawford of Design 408, the Council's Design Unit.

Special thanks are extended to Lewis Blake for researching and writing the main text and for co-ordinating and editing the work overall. His detailed knowledge and first-hand experience of the war years, together with his long and close acquaintance with Deptford and Lewisham, proved of great value at all stages in the work.

Ian Rawlinson

Chief Librarian and Arts Officer